On Matters of Liberation (I)
The Case Against Hierarchy

On Matters of Liberation (I)
The Case Against Hierarchy

Amardo Rodriguez

Purdue University

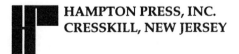 HAMPTON PRESS, INC.
CRESSKILL, NEW JERSEY

Printed in the United States of America.

Library of Congress Cataloging-in-Publication Data

Rodriguez, Amardo
    On matters of liberation : the case against hierarchy / Amardo
    Rodriguez
        p. cm. -- (The organizational experience in modern society)
    Includes bibliographic references and indexes.
    ISBN 1-57273-352-7 -- ISBN 1-57273-353-5
        1. Liberty. 2. Hierarchies. 3. Interpersonal relations. I. Title.
        II. Series

    HM1266.R63 2000
    323.44--dc21

                                                    00-059772

Hampton Press, Inc.
23 Broadway
Cresskill, NJ 07626

So far as I am aware, we are the only society on earth that thinks of itself as having risen from savagery, identified with a ruthless nature. Everyone else believes they are descended from gods. Even if these gods have natural representations, they nonetheless have supernatural attributes. Judging from social behavior, this contrast may well be a fair statement of the differences between ourselves and the rest of the world. In any case we make both a folklore and a science of our brutish origins, sometimes with precious little to distinguish them.

—Marshall Sahlins

Contents

Prologue

This is a book about liberation. In our day and age, both the possibility and the value of liberation are matters of profound societal debate. My position in this debate, which constitutes this book, is that *liberation is both possible and necessary* to being human. For humanity to fulfill its existential and spiritual aspirations, we must create human relationships that are devoid of coercion, domination, manipulation, and subordination. By existential aspirations or strivings, I mean any quality that is uniquely human. In other words, I will argue that human beings aspire to ends and ways of being that are uniquely human and that reveal our special relationship to the world. In this regard, I challenge the currently popular view that human beings are amoral, aspiritual, and not significantly different from other life forms. Such views are espoused across the political spectrum. Moreover, while they are given great play in public discourse, particularly in the news media and other nonacademic publications, they are also legitimized by growing numbers of academics.

The potential harm to our humanity demands that we challenge those that deny human existential and spiritual strivings. In this book, I join others who contest the trend toward ignorance and denial of our humanity; I hope to show the fundamental flaws in this line of thought. However, I have another more affirmative ambition in this project. I have written this book because I believe deeply that we have the potential and indeed the propensity to establish human relationships devoid of coercion, domination, subordination, and manipulation. I aim to show that human beings possess this liberatory potential.

I contend that the effects of hierarchy are real and perilous. Most importantly, hierarchy undercuts our moral capacity. In positing this thesis I am attempting to raise the stakes in the debates about hierarchy and liberation. I aim to contest what now passes for common ground. Moreover, I want to move discussions about hierarchy from the realm of political economy and organization—for example, the view that hierarchy undercuts productivity and efficiency—to the moral, existential, and spiritual realms. To make this shift, I will examine the worldviews that are implicit in debates about hierarchy and liberation. Worldviews are the bases of perspectives on the debates; they supply our truths; they equip us with our assumptions; they engender our particular hopes, fears, beliefs, and aspirations. Moreover, worldviews fashion the structure, process, and content of discussions and material practices; they determine ways of experiencing the world. In short, our beliefs, values, truths, hopes, fears, and so forth are the living embodiment of our worldview. I will argue that the most fundamental artifact of the dominant worldview is coercion. In this dominant paradigm, all truths, beliefs, and assumptions construct and sustain coercion as something *sacred*. Without the notion of coercion, the dominant worldview collapses.

I contend that coercion is the antithesis of human life. It undercuts our strivings toward liberation. In other words, coercion prevents us from forging deep and meaningful human relationships by engendering hierarchy, domination, manipulation, and subordination. Consequently, I will contest the argument that hierarchy is merely an arrangement of natural differences. Rather, hierarchy is a social arrangement based on coercion, domination, and subordination. I will also challenge the popular view that hierarchy is an artifact of evolutionary forces that are necessary for effective human organization, survival, and social evolution; in this argument, I will contest the correspondent notion that the dissolution of hierarchy will result in chaos, social devolution, and extinction.

Unfortunately, some of the more commonly understood shortcomings of hierarchy are fostering movements that threaten to coopt liberation. For example, this can be seen in "liberation management," the latest management approach that is now taught with much excitement in business and management schools. In efforts such as this, we encounter illusory challenges to hierarchy. In fact, stances such as "liberation management" actually mask the domination, manipulation, and subordination that occur in such supposedly nonhierarchical organizing schemes. Rather than fostering liberation, such schemes legitimize coercion and deepen distrust and suspicion of our humanity. Liberation is coopted when hierarchy is challenged superficially—when the underlying worldview that fosters hierarchy is unexamined.

Hierarchy undercuts the blossoming of our moral, existential, and spiritual strivings. The result is moral minimalism. We see this minimalism in the secularization of morality, which is epitomized by those who look to apes, chimpanzees, monkeys, bonobos, and other animals for our moral codes. The foundational notion in moral minimalism is the idea that human beings are amoral, aspiritual, and aexistential—essentially undifferentiable from our animal brethren. Those who view humanity in this way believe that human beings must be forcibly equipped with moral codes, such as those unleashed by free market forces. Moral minimalism stresses selfishness and autonomy. It assumes that the good, or moral behavior, is constituted by whatever appears to be good for oneself. Moral minimalism ignores or denies the essential relationship between human community and human being. All human relationships are conceived both descriptively and prescriptively as venues for manipulation and exploitation for individual gain. In this view, community is seen as a network of relationships that are configured by rational individuals attempting to gain; costs to others are considered only insofar as they might eventually interfere with personal gain.

Moral minimalism also stresses simplicity and universality. It requires that humans be easily equipped with simple moral codes. Such codes must be sufficiently simple and accessible so that they make for a moral currency that can be universally transferable. In this way of thinking, cooperation means nothing more than reciprocity; trust means nothing more than the capacity to exercise mutual retribution; commitment means nothing more than levels of investment of personal resources; and so forth.

To challenge these views, I will argue that human beings have both a capacity and a proclivity to develop deep and meaningful human relationships. It is only through the evolution of such relations that we become fully human and discover our existential and spiritual distinctiveness. It is our capacity and proclivity to develop such relationships that most fundamentally distinguishes us from apes, monkeys, bonobos, and other animals. Liberation represents the highest expression of our existential and spiritual strivings. It is an artifact of deep and meaningful human relations. Moreover, it represents the negation of coercion, domination, and subordination. Hence, liberation is our most profound moral obligation.

This book begins with a look at a few prominent expositions of liberation. The goal in these opening pages is to show that such writings commonly ignore the origins of coercion. As a consequence, what purports to be liberatory discourse fails to issue the necessary challenge to coercion and hierarchy, and it underanalyzes and misunderstands liberation. I will try to unpack the implications of these limitations. I will also offer an overview of the various perspectives within the scholarly community that posit coercion as truth. I will consider views in philosophy, law, psychology, biology, sociology, communication studies, and other areas of scholarship. I will focus narrowly on the most prominent arguments that the different traditions employ to support coercion as a truth. Throughout this discussion, I will focus on the origins of the assumptions, beliefs, and supposed truths that ground these most prominent arguments.

Following these analyses, I will examine the ways that worldviews construct our relations to the world and to each other. I will focus on the origins and nature of what I believe to be the dominant worldview. This is the worldview that grounds the scholarly perspectives on coercion. I will draw out the effects of this worldview for social and political theory and our everyday habits of being. The goal in this effort is to show that coercion is purely an artifact of the dominant worldview; it is an artifact of *man* rather than of nature or the gods.

I will also look at what I believe to be a nascent alternative worldview. To surmount hierarchy and coercion, we must experience a paradigm shift; a new worldview—a new consciousness—must appear. The nascent alternative worldview challenges bedrock propositions born of the dominant paradigm. It also gives us the opportunity to begin to look at the world noncoercively and to entertain the possibility of non-hierarchical ways of being. I will discuss bedrock propositions that distinguish the dominant and the emergent worldviews from each other, and I will highlight the consequences that accompany each stance. Ultimately, we must decide which worldview tells a better story, which gives a better account of the world, and which will better enable us to realize our humanity. I aim to show that the nascent, emerging worldview affords human relationships that will complement and foster the blossoming of our existential and spiritual strivings.

The book concludes with a discussion of the mechanics of nonhierarchical human relations. I will also show how the communicative and discursive practices that make and sustain hierarchy thwart our existential and spiritual strivings. However, the focus in this concluding chapter is on communicative practices that will give rise to nonhierarchical human relationships. This matter bears directly on question that motivates this project: What is the possibility and value of liberation? The significance of this question will be underscored by my argument that hierarchy is the antithesis of life.

1

Definitions
of Liberation

Most discussions of liberation hold coercion as a constant. Many discussions of liberation look carefully at the *mechanics* of coercion, but rarely do any look at its *origins*. Across theoretical, political, and religious spectrums, discussants assume that coercion is vital for the evolution of the good society. This disinterest in the origins of coercion, however, circumscribes our understanding of liberation. It forecloses discussions about the potential of human beings and the world. It blocks interrogation of our present relation to the world and each other, and what being human means. To hold coercion as a constant is to hold a worldview constant. The result is domination.

By contrast, to contest the legitimacy of coercion is to contest any notion of God that sanctions coercion; the view that hierarchy is an artifact of nature; the view that coercion is vital for the making of the good society; and, ultimately, what coercion tells us about being human. I contend that coercion thwarts what I refer to as our existential and spiritual strivings. In this way, coercion undercuts the forging of deep and meaningful human relations.

My position is rooted in a different assumptive ground than that which yields the dominant view of liberation. First, I assume that human beings are distinct from animals. Second, I assume that our humanity is by no means completely shaped by our discursive and material practices. Third, I assume that human beings have a distinct relation to the world, and that the nature of this relation resides within our existential and spiritual strivings. Liberation is the blossoming of such strivings.

Our attention turns now to an examination of a few prominent definitions of liberation. My goal is to show how coercion is left uninterrogated in these definitions. The theoretical, political, and ethical consequences of this deficiency will be addressed. I will focus on how this deficiency sustains a deep distrust and suspicion of human beings and the world. I then turn my attention to the nature of communication. I contend that communication represents an existential and spiritual striving. Looking at communication from this standpoint presents a fecund framework from which to look at liberation.

THE POLITICS OF DEFINITIONS

In my view liberation means becoming fully human through the forging of deep and meaningful human relations. Such relations are nonhierarchical. Liberation is also about the continuous evolution of new ways of being through the forging of deep and meaningful relations. Liberation ebbs and flows, as anything of human beings must. It reflects development and transformation.

Liberation means communion. Writers such as Cornel West and bell hooks view communion as the process of establishing a "beloved community." Other writers, such as Thomas Berry and Charlene Spretnak, view communion as returning to the unitive consciousness of the world, that is, recognizing that everything of the world is dynamically related. Both definitions foreground the relational nature of being human. I view communion similarly; *Communion is our entertwinedness with the cosmos and each other*. It is unselfishness and wholeness. The relational nature of being commits us to the well-being of each. This tie is existential, and hence uniquely human. A goal of this project is to show that these existential strivings can only blossom noncoercively. Thus, the possibility of liberation is an existential matter.

To posit liberation as communion is to contest the popular view of liberation as autonomy. Liberation as autonomy assumes an amoral, aexistential, and aspiritual view of human beings. It also assumes that human beings have no existential and spiritual relation to each other and the world. In addition, coercion is seen as vital to the good society so as to stop others from undercutting our liberation. Our distrust and suspicion of our humanity is left uninterrogated; similarly, the notions that coercion engenders, such as domination, subordination, and manipulation. In short, liberation as autonomy poses no threat to the status quo. In fact, this view of liberation actually further legitimizes the status quo by blocking scrutiny of the origins of hierarchy, such as coercion, domination, and manipulation. Unfortunately, however, this understanding of liberation remains the most common.

In *The Morality of Freedom*, Joseph Raz (1986), Professor of the Philosophy of Law at the University of Oxford and a Fellow of Balliol College, Oxford, gives us an argument for liberation as autonomy. In brief, the objective, according to Raz, is to construct a morality that will allow for the most autonomy without having that autonomy hamper the autonomy of others. This is technically referred to as a negative conception of freedom. It is about freedom *from* rather than freedom *to*. Raz writes, "Roughly speaking, one harms another when one's action makes the other person worse off than he was, or is entitled to be, in a way which affects his future well-being" (p. 414). It is, moreover, the responsibility of government to promote morality:

> Government should promote the moral quality of the life of those whose lives and actions they can affect. Does not this concession amount to a rejection of the harm principle? It does according to the common conception which regards the aim of freedom of governments to enforce morality. I wish to propose a different understanding of it, according to which it is a principle about the proper way to enforce morality. In other words I would suggest that the principle is derivable from a morality which regards personal autonomy as an essential ingredient of the good life, and regards the principle of autonomy, which imposes duties on people to secure for all the conditions of autonomy, as one of the foremost important moral principles. (p. 415)

It is also the function of government to bring coercion to bear on those who adversely transgress the autonomy of others. In this way, coercion is significant to Raz's definition of liberation. He writes:

> Autonomy is a matter of degree. A single act of coercion of not too serious nature makes little difference to a person's ability to lead an autonomous life. . . . Since individuals are guaranteed adequate rights of political participation in the liberal state and since such a state is guided by a public morality expressing concern for individual autonomy, its coercive measures do not express an insult to the autonomy of individuals. It is common knowledge that they are motivated not by lack of respect for individual autonomy but by a concern for it. After all, coercion can be genuinely for the good of the coerced and can even be sought by them. (pp. 156-157)

Raz gives us a secular definition of freedom. It is bereft of anything existential or spiritual. He says nothing about the virtues of freedom. Why freedom? Raz extricates freedom from being. He sees freedom as purely political. But by leaving coercion uninterrogated and entrusting government with engendering morality, he legitimizes certain notions of the world, our relation to each other, and what being human means. In other words, although Raz attempts to restrict his theory of liberation to the realm of the political, notions about the world and so forth are explicit. He assumes that human beings are amoral. It is the responsibility of government to engender morality. He also assumes that human beings have no existential or spiritual strivings for liberation. In his view, liberation is nothing more than a necessary condition for creating functional human relations. Consequently, Raz assumes that nothing is sacred about liberation.

Raz says nothing about the origins of his distrust of human beings. He assumes that coercion is vital to the good society. He also says nothing about why he believes human beings are amoral. Inattention to these issues reinforces the view that human beings are amoral. Because Raz views represent the dominant perspective, the status quo escapes interrogation. The origins of hierarchy also evade question.

To view hierarchy as a requirement of the good society reflects a deep distrust of the human condition. This distrust reflects the belief that human beings possess a proclivity for social devolution and chaos. It is my view, however, that hierarchy is born of *man*, specifically of a deep distrust of our humanity. Hierarchy reflects human relations that are constituted coercively by preventing the open expression of conflict. The open expression of conflict portends chaos and social devolution. In other words, without coercion, our proclivity for evil and chaos will be released and run amok. Hierarchy is born of this fear. In this way, hierarchy legitimizes coercion and domination. Conversely, hierarchy sustains and engenders a distrust of our humanity. It is a distrust that is recursively entwined with the perceived need for hierarchy. Accordingly, to look seriously at the origins and legitimacy of hierarchy demands also looking at the origins and legitimacy of coercion.

THE NATURE OF COERCION

I can find no discussion about the origins of coercion. By contrast, discussions about the legitimacy of coercion are plentiful. Most of these discussions focus on the moral, ethical, and legal considerations of coercion (e.g., Burawoy & Wright, 1990; Carr, 1988; Ehring, 1989; Gilbert, 1993; Hodson, 1983; Murray & Dudrick, 1995; Wertheimer, 1988; Young, 1986). The necessity of coercion is taken for granted. Absent from most discussions is any consideration of the effects of coercion on the physical, emotional, and spiritual well-being of human beings. Only behavior analysts give glancing attention to this matter. Bruce Waller (1990), author of *Freedom Without Responsibility*, argues that moral responsibility hinders freedom by legitimizing coercion. He argues that moral responsibility is the fundamental justification for coercion. He contends that coercion obstructs the cultivation of the temperament vital for autonomy. Simply put, coercion engenders dysfunctionality. Waller writes, "Holding people morally responsible not only blocks the most effective means of shaping individuals as they are now, but obscures the causes that shaped their current characters and behavior, and thus prevents effective programs that could change the large-scale social conditions that cause weak or undesirable characters" (1990, p. 140). Moreover, Waller contends that moral responsibility blocks deeper scrutiny into the conditions that shape behaviors. In this way, moral responsibility legitimizes inequality. It masks the fact that inequality restrains freedom. According to Waller:

> Freedom involves more than absence of prison walls; it requires
> the opportunity to exercise one's abilities, to develop one's skills,
> to learn to think carefully and critically, to have an influence on

events and society. For those who suffer from inadequate hous-
ing, poor education, inferior health care, and the other debilitating factors that are associated with poverty, living in freedom is
a cruel reminder of opportunities open to others. (1990, p. 202)

In *Coercion and Its Fallout*, Murray Sidman (1989) also argues
that coercion undermines liberation. He defines coercion as negative
reinforcement and punishment. Liberation, on the other hand, rests
with positive reinforcement. He writes:

Coercion is control through negative reinforcement and punishment. Positive reinforcement does control behavior, no less than
coercion does. But it can teach us new ways to act, or support
what we have already learned, without creating coercion's charac-
teristic byproducts—violence, aggression, oppression, depression,
emotional and intellectual rigidity, destruction of self and others,
hatred, illness, and general unhappiness. We usually punish in
order to prevent conduct that we consider harmful, dangerous, or
undesirable for other reasons. We justify coercion in the name of
education, civilization, morality, and self-defense. (p. 211)

The research does indeed show that—as far as promoting
desired behavior—positive reinforcement is superior to coercion.
Our society's fixation with coercion and punishment is contradictory
to the evidence and imperils the lives of those on the receiving end of
this fixation. Still, Sidman and Waller give us shallow descriptions of
both oppression and liberation. Both leave bedrock assumptions
uninterrogated. In reality, positive reinforcement is only a kinder and
gentler form of coercion. Sidman admits as much. Positive reinforcement still represents a form of constraint.

Sidman rarely address the question of human fallibility. His
perspective assumes that all human behavior is mechanical, the
effects of either positive or negative reinforcement. He assumes that
coercion is vital to the good society. In this way, Sidman and behavior analysts do have a distrust of our humanity. This distrust is evident when Sidman discusses noncontingent sharing:

In the future, with no intervention, what are the two levels to
expect from noncontingent sharing of all community resources,
and how will those levels come about? One tier of the welfare
society will contain producers, the other, parasites. People in the
worker class will engage interactively with their environment,

changing it, leaving their mark on it, building varied repertoires of conduct in response to natural and social contingencies; the workers will lead productive and potentially satisfying lives. Those in the parasite class will receive everything for nothing, lying on their backs with their mouths open for food, not interacting with and even alienated from their environments; the parasites will remain infantile and nonproductive. . . .

Parasites, with their basic needs satisfied, have little incentive to change. Why be a producer when others are willing to do it for you? How long will the producers remain productive under those circumstances? How long will they remain willing to share when they see the fruits of their labors siphoned off to those who get it just by fastening themselves on and waiting. (p. 204)

This argument is typical of persons who posit a distinct distrust and suspicion of our humanity. But again the research only shows that positive reinforcement is superior to negative reinforcement. That a society based on positive reinforcement will make for one superior to that based on negative reinforcement is a reasonable conclusion. On the other hand, however, casually assuming that this superior society is the most superior society that is humanly attainable—that is, it represents the full actualization of our potential—is simply beyond the bounds of good reasoning. To accept this kind of reasoning demands an unwillingness to question the assumptions that undergird Sidman's theory.

Sidman gives no consideration to the ethics of emergent forms of coercion. He believes that all reinforcements are readily discernible. In reality, however, coercion is becoming less and less discernible. Sidman never considers the coercion that comes with unobtrusive control, specifically the ethics of social control. What makes this omission significant is that unobtrusive coercion is now seen as the most effective and pervasive kind of coercion (Tompkins & Cheney, 1985). This coercion is as much unobtrusive as deceptive. It takes a myriad of forms. It produces unwitting consensual subordination. In short, coercion is coming to be understood as the illusion of real options. The options and choices that are available are narrow and predetermined. The best options never even appear and, consequently, are never given any kind of consideration. The predetermined options control the parameters of choice-making and thereby control action. Unobtrusive control sustains the otherwise unsupportable claim that persons can effectively and freely exercise volition. Carefully controlling the decisional premises and employing various framing devices accomplish this kind of deception.

Unobtrusive control also determines the outcomes of conflict by framing how the conflict unfolds and what are seen as reasonable outcomes. It manufactures consent and consensus by suppressing the open expression of conflict. In *Transforming Communication, Transforming Business*, Stanley Deetz, Professor of Communication, University of Colorado, Boulder, writes:

> Unobtrusive control as consent thus resides within the constitutive force of particular systems of representation: Consent arises with accepting discourses that constitute identities, social order, knowledge, and policy. In speaking (or really being spoken by) the discourse, a form of unwilled reproduction takes place and consent is implicitly manufactured and reaffirmed. In the discourse, the individual or stakeholder group loses its ability to engage in open productive communication, in which its own indeterminacy is placed in relation to an indeterminant outside, and instead engages in reproductive communication (information exchange), thus reproducing the dominant ordering and its stability. Important discussion is thus stopped . . . (1995, p. 128)

But identification probably achieves the most pernicious form of unobtrusive control. Identification means merging the self with the collective so that what is best for the collective is unreflexively seen as also what is best for the self. It entails subordinating the self through coercion, mostly under the guise that unity ultimately demands the suppression of differences. What is rarely recognized, however, is the actual subordination of self to the collective. For instance, most persons never notice when plural pronouns begin replacing singular pronouns. What is also rarely recognized is when the needs of the collective conflict with the needs of the self. The self becomes so tightly woven with the collective that self-reflection is difficult. It is the ability to exact superior control that is making unobtrusive control now so pervasive. Moreover, most persons now recognize the common ways that manipulation is packaged and know how to employ counter-tactics. Hence, a demand now exists for new kinds of less obvious packaging of control.

Viewing coercion as a necessity undercuts the justification for any rigorous scrutiny of the ethical concerns that unobtrusive coercion presents. On the other hand, nothing is fundamentally different about the kinds of moral and theoretical concerns that obtrusive and unobtrusive coercion present. If anything, the superior effectiveness—seeking total subordination of the self—of unobtrusive coercion merely sharpens our distrust of human beings. Sidman, however, is still theoretically hard pressed to complain about the effects of unobtrusive coercion. It seems from his theoretical standpoint that as long as the reinforcement is positive, everything is morally and ethically on the up and up. He may certainly find emergent forms of unobtrusive control repulsive, but he can neither contest the reasoning nor the moral legitimacy of such control. Moreover, by missing unobtrusive coercion, he cannot give us any substantive analysis of how society produces consent and obedient subordination. He cannot tell us anything about how a select group of human beings acquires the moral and ethical legitimacy to exercise positive reinforcement upon another group of human beings. What are the origins of the moral and ethical formulation that mediates this power? What is to stop the use of positive reinforcement for evil ends? Indeed, when our humanity becomes the sum of positive reinforcement, what does democracy mean? He also cannot tell us anything about this quest for total submission of the self or the effects of such an ambition on society. What will be the moral calculus? What would being human ultimately mean? The problem is that Sidman reduces all human relations to a network of causes and effects and reduces the well-being of the human condition to either the effects of positive or negative reinforcement. Positive reinforcement brings freedom, whereas negative reinforcement brings oppression. Morality is simply about whether the reinforcement is either positive or negative. Without any acknowledgment of an existential dimension to our humanity, morality is reduced to causality and utility. Liberation is the negation of negative reinforcement. His view of charity is revealing:

> Although it is sensible, and often satisfying, to share the fruits of success with the less fortunate, it is far more charitable to make that sharing noncontingent. Blind giving, in the name of humanitarianism, ensures that those who need charity because they have no productive skills will remain incapable. However distasteful we find the notion of controlling others through contingent giving, we control them anyway—inadvertently but just as effectively—by charity that is unrelated to anything they learn or accomplish. Noncontingent charity produces and perpetuates poverty. (p. 205)

But upon what research does Sidman base his arguments? Rodents. He constantly refers to research on rats. Evidently, Sidman sees no distinction between animals and human beings. Nothing existential or spiritual exists. This again is the popular presupposition. It reflects our deep distrust of human beings. Human beings are supposedly devoid of any natural capacity for goodness. *Man* is an animal. Consequently, the academy has no compunction about looking to animals to understand human behavior. What also emerges is a belief that order has to be created by man. Ultimately, man must be controlled. The remaining questions are simply who is in control and how need control be exercised. Popular discussions of liberation show this plainly. On the other hand, Raz, Sidman, and company never commit to examining the bedrock assumptions that uphold this popular view of human being. This deficiency, as I have argued, undermines rigor. It makes for bad theory. It also makes for bad politics. To hold coercion as a constant unobtrusively constrains theorizing about liberation by foreclosing on the possibility of new vistas for human beings and the world. In this way, it makes for the legitimacy of the status quo. It does nothing to unburden us of the deep fears on which the status quo thrives.

THE NATURE OF COMMUNICATION

To contend that our own hierarchical relations are comparable to the alphas and omegas of other animals is to claim that no fundamental differences exist between human beings and animals. But a fundamental distinction does exists. Only human beings possess a natural existential striving to bring meaning to bear on the world. Through communication human beings are humanized. Communication is the constitutive attribute of being human. This is the ontology of communication. Ontology deals with the nature of human existence. As Lee Thayer posits, "I am convinced that our failure to see communication for what it is—the source of our humanity and of everything else that is human—is not purely an intellectual shortcoming but a moral one" (1973, p. 130). Communication as meaning creation points to a sacred relation between being human and communication.

The popular view is that communication is about the transmission of messages. This is also the definition that pervades the academy. No doubt, animals do transact messages, but only human beings bring meaning to bear on the world. In short, the distinction between human beings and animals is missed when communication is seen as transmission, that is, messages between encoders and decoders. As a result, what is also missed is the existential and spiritual nature of human beings. In giving us a new vista of human beings, viewing communication as an existential and spiritual striving releases us from key assumptions that limit theorizing about liberation.

Communication is about the negotiation of shared meanings. New meanings afford new ways of being. Meaning creation processes are either functional or dysfunctional. Functional communication embraces ambiguity as something good and life affirming. It strives for transparency—reflecting an openness to the world. It is characterized by transparency, affirmation, continuity, and empathy. On the other hand, dysfunctional meaning creation processes reveal a deep fear of the world and other human beings. They are laden with deception, distrust, and punishment. Deception represents a fear of manipulation, subjugation, and exploitation. In sum, functional and dysfunctional communication represent different orientations to the world.

Dysfunctional communication engenders hierarchy by blocking the evolution of mutual transparency. Transparency is vital for the evolution of trust. Deception also thwarts empathy and compassion by engendering selfishness. The result is human relations woven with distrust and suspicion, which are manifest and managed by hierarchy. On the other hand, besides fostering trust, transparency hampers manipulation, subordination, and exploitation. Conversely, deception bedevils efforts to forge deep and meaningful human relations. It undercuts the vibrancy of meaning creation processes. It blocks the lucid evolution of new ways of being. Communication as meaning creation points to an actional view of human action. Human beings exercise volition. We make choices. We deliberately distort or clarify meanings. We fashion and construct our worlds through meanings.

Meaning is political. It reveals that human beings have the power to act upon the world and each other. It reflects our engagement with the world and each other. It reveals the condition of our humanity, the quality of our relations, and the nature of our relation to the world. Human beings are as much political as existential beings. According to Lee Thayer, "[T]he course and the quality and the destiny of human existence rest ultimately on what people are capable of expressing and of understanding" (1973, p. 134).

Communication as transmission or even expression gives us a shallow understanding of human beings. This definition disallows any serious consideration of a being with an existential dimension. Communication becomes simply transmission between purely physical beings for the satisfaction of purely utilitarian needs. No sacred relation between them is presupposed. Viewing communication as transmission reinforces the belief that human beings are autonomous beings who use communication purely for reasons of expression. This notion of autonomous being cultivates selfish behavior by privileging the needs of the person over the dyad or the collective.

Autonomous expression legitimizes competition. Negotiation is seen as a necessary evil, essential only for resolving clashing selfish ambitions. Negotiation connotes manipulation rather than cooperation. Whatever kind of cooperation appears is based on fear and distrust and is devoid of existential virtues. It is purely a political construct—born of political expediency. What follows is the evolution of a temperament that matches the encompassing context of suspicion and distrust. Compassion is suppressed. Deception is masked. Rationalizations that justify selfishness and deception become the norm. In fact, selfishness and deception become prescribed behavior.

Persons who look at communication as transmission also tend to make no distinction between human beings and animals. The understanding of liberation that emerges holds coercion as a constant. Liberation becomes a network of relations that afford maximum autonomy. Conversely, oppression represents anything that thwarts autonomy. No ethical and moral ground can be found to recognize let alone challenge the consequent selfishness and insensitivity to and distrust of fellow human beings. Presumably, such selfishness has no real effects on our humanity. In other words, there is no recognition between oppression and the undercutting of empathy, compassion, trust, and unselfishness.

An existential view of communication gives us different definitions of both liberation and oppression. To view communication existentially is to connect rather than to disconnect human beings. It acknowledges that the creation of our humanity occurs codeterminatively and, consequently, makes the shaping of each other's humanity a responsibility of others. In this way, other human beings are collaborators rather than competitors. Communication as negotiation demands a different orientation to our fellow human beings. It requires the development of a temperament born of cooperation rather than competition. Empathy is vital to the forging of this orientation. It is through empathy that our connection to other human beings is realized.

Viewing communication as transmission undermines the exercise of empathy. Our connectedness is downplayed. Relationships are reduced to networks. Moreover, conflict is perceived as dysfunctional, and a visceral aversion to conflict emerges. There is an unwillingness to confront conflict transparently. The result is human relations that reflect a deep fear of conflict, a general suspicion and distrust of, and anxiety toward other human beings, and a deep apprehension about exploring our own humanity.

Viewing communication as transmission also undermines the evolution of diversity. In this view, diversity connotes confusion and uncertainty. It represents the unknown. As diversity increases, so too do confusion and uncertainty. In turn, our fear of the unknown heightens our general suspicion of those who are presumably different. To deal with diversity is to deal with potential conflict, both of which are accomplished principally by avoidance. This is usually done through an array of unobtrusive measures and conflict suppression techniques that foster homogeneity. It is believed that homogeneity will control the uncertainty and potential confusion that diversity supposedly represents. A dogged determination emerges to torpedo anything that threatens to pollute our homogeneity and upset our cognitive stability. The suppression of conflict and the blocking of diversity, however, stop conflict from acting as a natural catalyst for growth and development. It is conflict that challenges human beings to look at the world differently and bring forth new ways of experiencing the world. In this way, conflict represents something existential. In short, conflict suppression through coercion is the antithesis of life. It blocks diversity and the blossoming of our humanity.

The end of the open expression of conflict and diversity is human relations based on coercion. In other words, the result is hierarchy. Hierarchy represents the suppression of conflict and diversity. Communication as transmission and expression sets up conflict as a clash between human beings with competing interests. To prevail, as competitors must, manipulation of others becomes paramount. General suspicion and distrust of others, as a matter of fact, are seen as vital safeguards against any assaults or ploys by a cunning and clever competitor. In short, any kind of vulnerability is seen as weakness. Trust becomes stability. It represents an arrangement between human beings—of equal skills or strength or capable of exacting fair amounts of punishment—to stop any kind of competition that could probably be equally detrimental to all participants. Trust is stripped of everything existential. It is supposedly an artifact of human evolution to aid survival against competitors of equal strength. Accordingly, even trust bespeaks coercion and manipulation. In fact, many social theorists now posit that trust is unnecessary for productive social relations. In *The Evolution of Cooperation*, a book that many critics contend makes a significant contribution to social theory, Robert Axelrod, Professor of Political Science and Public Policy at the University of Michigan, concludes:

> It is encouraging to see that cooperation can get started, can thrive in a variegated environment, and can protect itself once established. But what is most interesting is how little had to be assumed about the individuals or the social setting to establish these results. The individuals do not have to be rational: the evolutionary process allows the successful strategies to thrive, even if the players do not know why or how. Nor do the players have to exchange messages or commitments: they do not need words, because their deeds speak for them. Likewise there is no need to assume trust between the players . . . (1984, pp. 173-174)

Axelrod's findings are widely seen as recognizing the possibility of liberation when people are released from the oppressing effects of unnatural forces. Proponents of market forces enthusiastically contend that Axelrod's findings point to the end of government. (*The Wall Street Journal* gave the book a glowing review.) The coercion that is supposedly vital for making the good society can presumably be derived without government and other hindrances to market forces. It is, again, assumed that human beings are naturally selfish and deceitful and, as a result, human relations are best when they are arranged to exploit this truth. Other prominent scholars contend that this is the nature of our genes and that Axelrod's conclusions are only confirmatory. When one examines the definition of communication that persons siding with Axelrod employ, this is a logical conclusion. Communication is an artifact of being that evolved solely for reasons of coordination and survival.

Axelrod vacillates on what his findings mean politically. The connection to Charles Darwin's theory of natural selection is also downplayed. On the other hand, the way Axelrod casually reduces human beings to purely selfish and autonomous beings is laden with distinct biases and prejudices that bear directly on how his research is cast and the findings interpreted. It is important to note, however, that being nice, fair, forgiving, and vulnerable characterized the most successful strategy that actors employed in his research. However, Axelrod is convinced that this is merely further proof of human beings having a selfish nature. What is also noteworthy is that this propensity to be nice, fair, and so forth emerged with actors who had no opportunity to communicate and thereby establish any relationship at all with other actors. Axelrod never considers communication a significant mediating factor in human action. He misses, as a result, the extent to which human relationships shape motives and action. Apparently, for Axelrod, relationships mean nothing. This view is simply wrong. It is contrary to our own experiences.

Axelrod also makes no consideration for culture. It is a revealing omission. Selfishness is supposedly the sine qua non of human motivation and action. Nothing apparently moderates our selfish ambitions. Neither cultures nor relationships fashion our humanity. These omissions show how Axelrod's view of the human condition foregrounds his research and overly narrows—to the point of distortion—what the findings mean. However, other research using the exact protocol that Axelrod used shows compellingly that culture is a significant factor. I will return to all of this later. The present point is that to look at communication as merely transmission and expression is to strip our humanity of everything existential. This results in dysfunctional ways of being and the dysfunctional human relations that is hierarchy. In these many ways, the beliefs, assumptions, truths, values, and other discursive practices evolving from this view of communication thwart our becoming fully human.

SUMMARY AND CONCLUSION

Hierarchy grips us. Our common notions of God sanction hierarchy. God presumably punishes those who transgress *his* laws and defy *his* wishes. Most religions posit this explicitly. We are taught that human beings possess a proclivity for chaos and evil. The corollary is a belief that coercion is vital for the making of the good society. As a result, our relations to the world and each other are shaped hierarchically. Consequently, to contest hierarchy as a truth is to contest many deeply held and sacred notions about our relation to the world and each other, and what being human means.

A lack of rigor constrains our understanding of liberation. Bedrock assumptions are left uninterrogated. Our distrust and suspicion of our humanity are left uninterrogated. In this way, also unexamined are all the notions that coercion engenders, such as domination, subordination, and manipulation. An amoral, aexistential, and aspiritual view of human beings is presupposed, which assumes that human beings have no existential and spiritual relation to each other and the world. Autonomy emerges as liberation. But the notion of liberation as autonomy poses no threat to the status quo. It actually further legitimizes the status quo by blocking scrutiny of the origins of hierarchy. Consequently, liberation as autonomy blocks any deep exploration and consideration of the notion of liberation. New vistas of human beings and the world are suppressed. The result is domination.

Coercion thwarts our existential and spiritual strivings. Communication is a manifestation of such strivings. In addition, coercion engenders hierarchy by engendering distrust, suspicion, and fear. The results are dysfunctional ways of being. In this way, coercion undercuts the forging of deep and meaningful relations. However, engendering hierarchy and ending hierarchy are different matters. It is common to hear calls for the end of coercion from quarters claiming vociferously that hierarchy is natural and vital for the making of the good society. Arguably, all I have shown so far is that bedrock assumptions have been left uninterrogated and that meaning creation distinguishes human beings from animals. Nothing about either argument really represents an end to hierarchy. It is yet to be shown, as I claim, that the origins of hierarchy are purely social. Indeed, I will address the endless arguments that claim differently. Accordingly, the discussion now proceeds to an examination of the many arguments positing that hierarchy is an artifact of nature that is vital to the good society.

2

The Origins
of Hierarchy

Our deep distrust of our humanity is reinforced constantly by religion, philosophy, society, family, and the academy. It is difficult for most of us to fathom nonhierarchical human relations. For without hierarchy, religion threatens us with damnation, government threatens us with anarchy, society threatens us with lawlessness, capital threatens us with underdevelopment, and education threatens us with regression to animality. In short, theologians, philosophers, and scholars have long postulated that hierarchy represents the natural order of the world. The arguments are many—too many to review, but constant to all the arguments is a deep distrust of human beings. Hierarchy supposedly controls our evil and destructive ways and makes for better human beings. It is natural and functional. In *The Politics of Social Knowledge*, Larry D. Spence (1978) compellingly argues that the inevitability of hierarchy assumes the inevitability of widespread social ignorance. We believe that all human beings lack the motivation, character, and intelligence to sustain nonhierarchical relations. Indeed, this belief is so embedded within Western thought and consciousness that our political and educational institutions refuse to take seriously facts and arguments that contest this belief. Hierarchy has evolved to mythology. To even question the legitimacy of hierarchy is to risk being labeled a fool or a utopian. Spence writes:

> The evolution of a science of humanity has been blocked by persistent assumptions about the nature of the human species and human societies. The species has been judged as wanting in motivation, character, and intelligence. . . . A second entrenched and destructive assumption is the conviction that human societies are inevitably hierarchical. Both assumptions have assumed the structure and power of myths in that there are no facts known or imaginable that can falsify them, no events or actions that could result in their modification. . . . Find a group of cooperating producers without structured positions of domination and you will have only failed to see the hidden hierarchy and the totally conformist nature of their behavior. The combined myths of unreliable men and women enlightened and ennobled by an omniscient hierarchy of administrators is so much an implicit part of the perspective of the social investigator as to be immune to minimal criticism. To challenge these myths is to undergo the risks involved in taking stands against the political and academic institutions of our age. (p. 1)

Our attention turns now to a few of the prominent arguments posited by proponents of hierarchy. We begin with a cursory look at a few arguments. We then look critically at different arguments that the academy posits. This will occupy most of our attention. The arguments span theoretical, ideological, and political interests. We aim to show that such arguments lack rigor. In other words, the academy has yet to offer a compelling argument for hierarchy. On the other hand, the theoretical cover that the academy provides to hierarchy legitimizes the status quo by blocking serious consideration of non-hierarchical relations. Our goal is to press this claim forward.

HIERARCHY, CHRISTIANITY AND GOD

Hierarchy finds legitimation across theoretical, philosophical, and spiritual interests. Proponents tend to have no problems finding common ground. In *Power: A New Social Analysis*, Bertrand Russell said:

Human beings find it profitable to live in communities, but their desires, unlike those of bees in a hive, remain largely individual; hence arises the difficulty of social life and the need for government [read coercion]. For, on the one hand, government is necessary: without it, only a very small percentage of the population of civilized countries could hope to survive, and that in a state of pitiable destitution. But, on the other hand, government involves inequalities of power, and those who have most power will use it to further their own desires as opposed to those of ordinary citizens. Thus anarchy and despotism are alike disastrous, and some compromise is necessary if human beings are to be happy. (1995, p. 139)

John Stuart Mill, whose essay *On Liberty* is a canon among liberatory offerings, feels similarly. McKercher observes:

In many ways Mill's words are filled with pessimism because he believes that human beings cannot be free and secure without a comprehensive system of law which will allow the individual . . . to pursue self-development in concert with the rest of society. We cannot doubt that Mill believed that coercion was necessary to prevent even greater evils; and this coercion was to be enforced by groups within the society, which were by various means designated spokesmen for the society in general. (1989, p. 59)

Rene Girard, the famous French scholar, believes that hierarchy is necessary to stop the destructive ways of our violent nature. In other words, hierarchy is purely an artifact of necessity, without which *man* is damned. He refers to hierarchy as noninstinctive restraint. Girard also believes that our violent nature gave rise to the origin of language and institutions. Similarly, in an essay entitled *Communication, Conflict, and Culture*, David Mortensen, Professor of Communication Arts at the University of Wisconsin-Madison, posits that language, culture, and communication coevolved to end the violent conflict that stems from our endowed capacity for strife and conflict. Mortensen contends that "Struggle and strife permeate relations between human beings in ways that are peculiar to the species" (1991, p. 275). Robert Weissberg, author of *Political Tolerance*, puts the matter the following way:

Civil society must, by its intrinsic character, impose limits, and may demand incarceration or death. What precisely is condemned, and by what instrumentality, cannot be deduced logical-

ly or historically. It all depends on historical circumstances, and
the inherent murkiness of dividing lines makes implementation
controversial. But such dilemmas, imprecisions, and hazy bound-
aries are not an invitation to the blank-check type of tolerance
routinely invoked in the modern tolerance literature. (1999, p. 94)

Proponents of hierarchy commonly contend that it is an arti-
fact of history and progress. For instance, Michael Zimmerman,
Professor of Philosophy at Tulane University and author of
Contesting Earth's Future, has no qualms asserting, "There is no deny-
ing the fact . . . that encouraging people to treat each other with
respect, justice, and compassion is . . . indebted to Christianity and to
Western European modernity" (1994, p. 274). In *Slouching Towards
Gomorrah*, Robert Bork argues similarly:

What needs to be said is that no other culture in the history of
the world has offered the individual as much freedom, as much
opportunity to advance; no other culture has permitted homosexuals, non-whites, and women to play ever-increasing roles in
the economy, in politics, in scholarship, in government. What
needs to be said is that American culture is Eurocentric, and it
must remain Eurocentric or collapse into meaninglessness.
Standards of European and American origin are the only possible standards that can hold our society together and keep us a
competent nation. If the legitimacy of Eurocentric standards is
denied, there is nothing else . . . The alternative to Eurocentrism,
then, is fragmentation and chaos. (1996, p. 311)

In *A History of Christianity*, Paul Johnson, writes:

Certainly, mankind without Christianity conjures up a dismal
prospect. The record of mankind *with* Christianity is daunting
enough. . . . [T]here is a cruel and pitiless nature in man which is
sometimes impervious to Christian restraints and encourage-
ments. But without these restraints, bereft of these encourage-
ments, how much more horrific the history of these last 2,000
years must have been! Christianity has not made man secure or
happy or even dignified. But it supplies hope. It is a civilizing
agent. It helps cage the beast. It offers glimpses of real freedom. . . .
In the last generation, with public Christianity in headlong retreat,
we have caught our first, distant view of a de-Christianized world,
and it is not encouraging. . . . Man is imperfect without God.
Without God, what is he? (1976, p. 517)

But history gives us good reason to challenge the belief that coercion is vital for the making of the good society. History compellingly shows that the most heinous acts of human devolution and bestiality appear within a context of coercion and hierarchy. Hitler's Germany, Franco's Spain, Stalin's Russia, Mao's China, and Mussolini's Italy are all distinguishable by the exclusive use of coercion to build the good society. In fact, history has yet to reveal any society that is without a deep distrust of human beings that is comparatively bestial to those that characterized the world this century. Indeed, history plainly suggests that coercion and hierarchy are artifacts of social devolution rather than social evolution. The problem, however, is that this suggestion clashes with our deep belief that Western society evidences the most progress, the most sophistication, that is, the least amount of human savagery in human history. But modern times give us reason enough to question the legitimacy of coercion. In fact, history seems to be nudging us toward this questioning. We must now seize the opportunity to consider definitions of liberation beyond simply quantity and quality of coercion.

NURTURE AND NATURE

The academy is nearly unanimous in the view that hierarchy is vital for the evolution of the good society. It also now increasingly houses the most vocal proponents of coercion and hierarchy. Again, support spans theoretical, political, and scholarly interests. Even academics who call for the end of hierarchy assume or assert that coercion is the order of the world. We will look at prominent arguments under the labels of *nurturists* and *naturists*. Many will no doubt reject this approach as a dated and vulgar dichotomy. However, I do not adopt this pair of opposing terms as a means of organizing and grouping all relevant perspectives. Even a cursory review demonstrates a cacophony of viewpoints: modernism, neomodernism, postmodernism, ecological postmodernism, structuralism, poststructuralism, positivism, neopositivism, anarchism, syndicalist anarchism, communitarian anarchism, communism, functionalism, socialism, pragmatism, ecofeminism, deep ecology, radical ecology, social ecology, liberalism, conservatism, neoconservatism, critical theory, and many other too numerous to mention. Clearly, no simple dichotomy can capture the diversity in these views. However, it is just as clear that theorizing about the relative importance of nurture and nature is central to these literatures. I should also note that only a few naturists completely reject environmental factors. The controversy among naturists is about the extent to which environment is a determining factor. However, let us begin by considering how a few prominent nurturists look at coercion and hierarchy.

HIERARCHY AS NURTURE

Nurturists posit that our humanity is purely a discursive creation. Ways of verbalizing, writing, moving, text, cognition, argumentation, and representation construct and constrain our humanity. In *Frameworks of Power*, Stewart Clegg, Professor of Sociology at the University of New England, Armidale, explains the position well:

> Identity is never regarded as being given by nature; individuality is never seen as fixed in its expression . . . admits of no rational, unified human being, nor class nor gendered subject which is the locus or source of expression of identity. Membership in a category, as a particular subject, is contingent, provisional, achieved not given. Identity is always seen as a process. . . . [O]ne can only be seen to be something in relation to some other thing. Identity is always defined in terms of difference, rather than as something intrinsic to a particular person or category of experience, such as worker, wife, woman, or whore. (1989, p. 151)

Discursive openness theoretically represents the negation of oppression. Most theorists of this philosophical persuasion seek to deconstruct discursive practices that oppress and constrain our being. Liberation becomes the deconstruction of those practices and narratives that block open expression of conflict, diversity, and the full expression of our humanity. In other words, liberation is negative freedom, freedom from such practices and narratives. The contention is that oppression results from both systematically distorted communication and discursive closure. It is generally characterized by lack of openness, privileging of certain experiences and viewpoints, and subtly blocking, suppressing, and thwarting the open development of understanding between and among persons. According to Stanley Deetz, oppression occurs when a select group of persons blocks exploration of such practices so as to benefit advantageously at the cost of others (usually the majority). Deetz states, "When discussion is thwarted, a particular view of reality is maintained at the expense of equally plausible ones, usually to someone's advantage" (1992, p. 188). This is a discursive conceptualization of oppression. Moreover, according to Dennis Mumby, Professor of Communication, Purdue University:

> Interpreted positively, the move away from a subject/speaker-centered conception of communication (in which subjectivity is not taken as problematic to be explored) permits us to reconceptualise subjectivity as discursively constructed and hence open to change. In this sense, communication is not conceived as the effect of the speaking subject. Indeed, from a [nurturist] perspective, it is more appropriate to argue that subjectivity is an effect of communication. (1997, pp. 20-21)

If, however, all of our humanity is a discursive creation, from what ground or position do humans act? In other words, what becomes of agency? According to Mumby:

> No one would deny that, for the most part, social actors have particular intentions in mind when communicating. But if we focus on intent as the defining characteristic of communication, then we fail to recognize that communicative acts always occur within the context of larger social relations that exist independently of any intent that specific communicators have. . . . Intent does not arise from nowhere—it is a product of our condition as interpellated subjects. . . . Intention is an element of the communication process, but it is an element that is always mitigated and contextualized by the way discursive practices shape us as subjects. (p. 21)

However, according to Stanley Fish, Arts and Sciences Professor of English and Professor of Law at Duke University, and a prominent proponent of the discursive model, no ground really exists. Agency is a discursive illusion. Fish concedes:

> [T]here is always a gun at your head. Sometimes the gun is, in literal fact, a gun; sometimes it is reason, an assertion whose weight is inseparable from some already assumed purpose; sometimes it is a desire . . . sometimes it is a need you already feel. . . . Whatever it is, it will always be a form of coercion, of an imperative whose source is an interest which speaks to the interest in you. And this

leads me to a second aphorism: not only is there always a gun at your head; *the gun at your head is your head*; the interests that seek to compel you are appealing and therefore pressuring only to the extent they already live within you, and indeed *are* you. In the end we are always self-compelled, coerced by forces—beliefs, convictions, reasons, desires—from which we cannot move one inch a way. (1989, p. 520, emphasis in original)

Mumby believes that looking at the human condition as an artifact of discursivity actually expands our understanding of liberation. He writes:

The conception of the subject *as the effect of communication* permits us to focus on the extent to which the *social actor is a product of the practices of power and domination.* . . . Within such a framework we can recognize the extent to which social actors are the *site* of discourses that attempt to create and fix subjectivities in a particular fashion. Postulating communication as subjectless is thus not an attempt to deny that *real social actors* communicate intentionally with one another. Rather, it helps us to recognize the extent to which intent is possible only because we are always situated within systems of discourse that precede and exceed us as communication. (p. 22, emphasis mine)

But without volition and any kind of spiritual ground, what morality guides human affairs? What will be the objective moral calculus that will condemn, say, slavery? What can possibly be the morality of subjectless communication? Or, would human relations exist without any morality? This kind of moral agnosticism is troubling. What might stop the majority or those with the most resources from persecuting a certain minority group? What would be the argument for equality and liberation? What is to stop the abuse or use of the discursive model to correct any behavior that a dominant group defines as deviant and a threat to the good society? Indeed, what would be the moral and ethical arguments against hierarchy and coercion? Again Fish concedes, "Does might make right? In a sense the answer I must give is yes, since in the absence of a perspective independent of interpretation some interpretive perspective will always rule by having won out over its competitors" (1989, p. 10).

Prominent proponents of the discursive view contend that opponents have a fixation with *totalizing* moral codes. But undoubtedly a rigorous moral calculus is vital to claim that oppression of any person or group is morally and ethically wrong. Without any agency or moral ground, all that is left is moral relativism. Human beings are cast as without moral strivings. We are devoid of anything existential. Accordingly, to posit human beings as purely a discursive creation precludes any way of grappling with and theorizing about such existential notions as passion, growth, development, transformation, and, ultimately, liberation. According to Noam Chomsky:

> If in fact humans are indefinitely malleable, completely plastic beings, with no innate structures of mind and no intrinsic needs of a cultural or social character, then they are fit subjects for [oppression]. . . . Those with some confidence in the human species will hope this is not so and will try to determine the intrinsic human characteristics that provide the framework for intellectual development, the growth of moral consciousness, cultural achievement, and participation in a free community. (1987, p. 154)

The corollary of moral relativism is nihilism. Put another way, viewing the human condition as purely a product of discursive and material practices engenders hopelessness. As Murray Bookchin astutely observes:

> The more one feels disempowered about the human condition and bereft of social commitment, the more one becomes cynical and thereby captive to the prevailing social order. To the extent that hope and belief in progress are lost, a disarming relativism, ahistoricism, and ultimately nihilism replace any belief in the objectivity of truth, the reality of history, and the power of reason to change the world (1995, pp. 175-176)

If, moreover, human beings are purely discursive beings, what becomes of responsibility? The fact is, without agency or ground, responsibility has no location. If again human beings are purely discursive beings, then responsibility should logically rest with discursivity. But this shifts responsibility away from human beings. It would now rest with the discursive world. A problem also arises with regard to explanations of the effects of oppression, such as pain and suffering. In a discursive world, such effects would have to be seen as purely social constructions. If human beings are devoid of any essences, nothing is really oppressed. In short, the effects of oppression are reduced to nothing but social constructions. But this strips oppression of all meanings and thereby trivializes the suffering of victims. As Peter McLaren and Peter Lankshear point out:

> Knowledge can be depotentiated and stripped of its emancipatory possibilities if it is acknowledged only as a form of textualization. Moreover, such a facile treatment of discourse can lead to the subject's encapsulation in the membranes of his or her rationalizations, leading to a soporific escape from the pain and sensations of living, breathing, human subjects. (1994, p. 7)

Proponents of the discursive view posit no explicit distrust and suspicion of human beings. But viewing humans as purely discursive beings makes for a model that foregrounds coercion. Fish erases any doubts about this conclusion. In his view, liberation is about degrees of coercion. Neither a moral calculus nor a means of explaining progress and social evolution is offered. All that remains is nihilism and moral relativism. However, by no means have proponents compellingly shown that human beings are amoral beings. No compelling argument that humans are completely devoid of any ground is ever given. Still, by promoting the view of an amoral being, proponents lend legitimacy to any kind of human artifact that would guard amoral beings from one another. Any such artifact must obviously function coercively because no ground exists to appeal to. In the end, then, the discursive position damns human beings to coercion and relations laden with distrust and suspicion.

HIERARCHY AS NATURE

The ancient Greeks believed that human beings possessed different natures. Plato believed that persons had different souls, either gold, silver, or bronze. He also believed that society should be arranged accordingly, that is, hierarchically. Pythagoras, on the other hand, held that, "There is a good principle that has created order, light and man, and a bad principle which has created chaos, darkness and women." He, too, believed that society should be arranged accordingly. Of course, ancient Greek society was arranged hierarchically. Probably the most well-known notion embodying the naturist perspective is that of original sin. However, I restrict my attention to the propositions of modern naturists—nearly all of whom are vociferous proponents of Charles Darwin's natural selection theory. I do this because this theory is increasingly shaping and legitimizing a lot of the discourses about the good society. According to Daniel Dennett, Distinguished Arts and Sciences Professor and Director of the Center for Cognitive Studies at Tufts University, "The evidence for evolution pours in, not only from geology, paleontology, biogeography, and anatomy (Darwin's chief sources), but of course from molecular biology and every other branch of the life sciences. To put it bluntly but fairly, anyone today who doubts that the variety of life on this planet was produced by a process of evolution is simply ignorant—inexcusably ignorant . . ." (1995, p. 46). I aim only to afford a working understanding of the different positions among modern naturists. I focus specifically on the works by Richard Dawkins, E. O. Wilson, Richard Wright, Willard Gaylin and Bruce Jennings, and a few other representative works of this tradition. I also accent only the various arguments that deal with hierarchy and coercion.

Sociobiology

Many segments of the scholarly community increasingly posit no distinction between us and animals. We are seen as simply evolved animals. Stephen Jay Gould, Professor of Geology and Zoology at Harvard University, even claims that human beings were an accident of evolutionary processes. In *The Human Difference*, Alan Wolfe, University Professor and Professor of Sociology at Boston University, observes:

> There is, then, a set of ideas that can be found in all fields of con-
> temporary intellectual endeavor, whether viewed as part of the
> sciences, the humanities, or a mixture of both. These ideas tran-
> scend any political identification, sometimes appearing among
> those on the left . . . at other times among those on the right. . . .
> The contours of emerging cosmology are anything but fixed, and
> borrowings across disciplines have recently been noticed. Yet
> when all the strands are added together, a fundamental challenge
> to one of the two principles that shaped Enlightenment thought
> about humanism can be discovered. It is not equality within the
> human species that is being challenged. It is instead the notion
> that we ought to accept inequality between the human and non-
> human species. Humans have no special qualities and deserve no
> special place. . . . It is time to take our place as one of nature's
> minor miracles, no different in degree from all the other minor

miracles found therein. Any intellectual enterprise premised on
the assumption that humans occupy a privileged place in the
world begins, these days, with the burden of doubt. . . . The intellectual conditions that gave rise to a belief in the special and distinct characteristics of the human self and human society are
weaker than at any point in the past century. (1993, p. 15)

Most scholars who posit such views claim that all life forms
have a common nature that determines behavior. Volition is downplayed. The quarrel among modern naturists centers on what determines human behavior. The competing positions are biological and
psychological. Richard Dawkins, Charles Simonyi Professor of the
Public Understanding of Science at Oxford University, makes his
position explicit on the back cover of his bestseller, *The Selfish Gene*,
"Our genes made us. We animals exist for their preservation and are
nothing more that their throwaway survival machines. The world of
the selfish gene is one of savage competition, ruthless exploitation,
and deceit." This is the gist of the book. Developing this thesis in the
opening pages, Dawkins says:

I shall argue that a predominant quality to be expected in a successful gene is ruthless selfishness. This gene selfishness will
usually give rise to selfishness in individual behavior. . . . Much
as we might wish to believe otherwise, universal love and the
welfare of the species as a whole are concepts that simply do not
make evolutionary sense. (1989, p. 2)

It is supposedly our genes that contain the forces of evolution. According to Dawkins, animal and plant forms have evolved to
do the bidding of genes. He refers to such forms as survival
machines. The mainstream position is that natural selection is about
competition between and among species. Dawkins explicitly refuses
to take a position on the nature/nurture controversy. He contends
that neither his politics nor morality is premised on selfishness: "Let
us try to *teach* generosity and altruism, because we are born selfish.
Let us understand what our selfish genes are up to, because we may
then at least have the chance to upset their designs, something that
no other species has ever aspired to do" (p. 3). In the latest edition of
the book, Dawkins sketches a calculus for how this could be accomplished within the framework of our selfish nature. I will attend to
this matter shortly; right now I am concerned with the rationale for
Dawkins' stance. Why the need for this unnatural privileging of

unselfishness? If selfishness is the catalyst of progress and evolution, why upset a good thing?

Dawkins never explains why this emergent need exists to teach unselfishness or the reasons to counter selfishness. All of this raises another question: Why restrict any upsetting just to human beings? Why cannot unselfishness also work in a superior fashion for birds and other survival machines? In other words, what distinguishes our faith from that of birds and other survival machines? After all, Robert Trivers claims in the foreword of the first edition of Dawkins' book—which is noticeably absent from the last—that, "There exists no objective basis on which to elevate one species above the other" (p. v). Dawkins never addresses such questions. It is a revealing omission. He is, however, convinced that human beings can and must thwart selfishness. He writes:

> I am trying to build up the idea that animal behavior, altruistic or selfish, is under the control of genes in only an indirect, but still very powerful, sense. By dictating the way survival machines and their nervous systems are built, genes exert ultimate behavior. But the moment-to-moment decisions about what to do next are taken by the nervous system. Genes are the primary policy-makers; brains are the executives. But as brains became more highly developed, they took over more and more of the actual policy decisions, using tricks like learning and simulation in doing so. The logical conclusion to this trend, not yet reached in any species, would be for the genes to give the survival machine a single overall policy instruction: do whatever is best to keep us alive. (p. 60)

This conclusion only raises other questions. Dawkins points to an evolution away from selfishness. The suggestion is that this would be a good thing. On the other hand, Dawkins admits that genes that foster altruism are yet to be found. What has supposedly evolved so far that could foster altruism is *communication*. Dawkins contends that through communication human beings can learn and eventually develop genes that are likely to act altruistically rather than selfishly. However, as the root of all evolutionary behavior is survival, communication reeks with selfishness and deception. On the other hand, however, Dawkins posits that although survival machines are ceaselessly trying to profit selfishly, mutual recognition eventually emerges between and among survival machines that selfishness could threaten the survival of all. Simply put, natural selection demands that genes constantly weigh the cost of selfishness and survival. It is out of this weighing, according to Dawkins, that trust emerges. In other words, trust emerges from fear, distrust, and suspicion. It reflects the recognition of retribution. Accordingly, without the threat of retribution, trust collapses. In Dawkins' theory, trust has no existential and spiritual origins.

Dawkins claims that all genes are continually assessing the cost of selfishness against the chances of survival. Selfishness demands that I seek the elimination of all my rivals for resources and mates. On the other hand, such action could destroy alliances that are probably necessary to sustain survival against other foes. Moreover, survival could also be threatened when trying to destroy or exploit rivals. Thus survival of the fittest demands that genes temper selfishness and other acts of deceit. In sum, the virtues of cooperation are recognized, the most prevalent form of which is symbiosis. This occurs when different species perform different tasks for each other. Another significant kind of cooperation is hierarchical ordering between and among those with different strengths. So rather than deal with the heightened possibility of annihilation through competition with others who are bigger and stronger, a superior option would be to become a subservient ally. According to Dawkins, this is the natural origin of hierarchy. In other words, hierarchy, too, is born of fear, distrust, and suspicion. It is a natural arrangement between weak and strong that is vital for the evolution of cooperation. The fact that this arrangement allows both groups to coexist peacefully supposedly represents the good of hierarchy. Subordination, after all, still ensures survival and potential perpetuation of the genes of the weakest groups. Hence, Dawkins views hierarchy as something functional, natural, and moral.

The recognition of cooperation eventually evolves to what Maynard Smith refers to as an *evolutionary stable strategy* (ESS). (Dawkins discusses Smith's work at great lengths.) It is the recognition that my own behavior is likely to be met by a copy of that very behavior. ESS is essentially the calculus that protects all participants from the selfish yearnings of others. The evolution of mechanisms to thwart selfishness make for social evolution. Central to this process are notions of punishment and the threat of punishment. According to Dawkins, the stability and further evolution of cooperative behavior depends on our ability to punish those who seek to profit from the vulnerability that is at the center of any cooperative arrangement. In this way, any party attempting to profit disadvantageously will be dissuaded from doing so because losses could outweigh potential gains. Out of this stability that is achieved through the threat of mutual destruction, cooperation evolves and blossoms. (Axelrod's research is seen as confirming the validity of ESS.) Also facilitating this natural evolution of cooperation is what Dawkins refers to as *memes*, that is, the transmission of distinguishing cultural features. In short, Dawkins' theory has a cultural component.

Dawkins gives us a secular definition of cooperation. It is selfishness (and coercion and retribution) rather than unselfishness that makes for cooperation. In fact, selfishness seems to be the vital component. In this way, Dawkins' theory of cooperation is a natural outgrowth of natural selection forces rather than any kind of antithesis. Ruthless selfishness lead to the evolution of cooperation. Fear of retribution and mutual annihilation propels the process. Ruthless selfishness ultimately leads to the evolution of *memes* and other habits of being that reflect cooperation. All of this again raises the question of why Dawkins now wishes to transgress against the forces of natural selection by teaching unselfishness. Further, the research that Dawkins uses to sketch his theory of cooperation—especially, Axelrod's—explicitly states that selfishness is vital to the evolution of cooperation. Conversely, social devolution is likely with the end of selfishness. This notion also sustains Dawkins' view that genes are the primary policy-makers of human behavior.

It seems that Dawkins confuses the negation of competition with the elimination of selfishness. Natural selection theory, after all, seems amenable to a union of cooperation and ruthless selfishness. Moreover, the concept of ruthless selfishness can be used to produce an *objective* account of cooperation. This is something that is attractive to persons who want objective truths. In fact, many such persons are attracted to Darwin's natural selection theory for this very reason. The problem is that Dawkins makes no compelling argument as to why selfishness is dysfunctional. Indeed, his theory is sustained by the concept of selfishness. He believes that selfishness is vital to the making of the good society. He speculates about how competition can end deviancy. It appears that Dawkins' equivocality is unnecessary. He seems better off proclaiming the supposed virtues of natural selection theory.

This, as a matter of fact, is exactly what E. O. Wilson, Frank B. Baird Professor of Science and Curator in Entomology, Harvard University, does. Wilson is the original articulator of *sociobiology*, the relatively new field of study that attempts to offer a biological basis for all social behavior by relying on natural selection theory. Like Dawkins, E. O. Wilson acknowledges the efficacy of environment.

However, Wilson firmly believes that selfishness fashions social behavior. In *On Human Nature*, which won a Pulitzer Prize, Wilson writes:

> Can the cultural evolution of higher ethical values gain a direction and momentum of its own and completely replace genetic evolution? I think not. The genes hold culture on a leash. The leash is very long, but inevitably values will be constrained in accordance with their effects on the human gene pool. The brain is a product of evolution. Human behavior—like the deepest capacities for emotional response which drive and guide it—is the circuitous technique by which human genetic material has been and will be kept intact. Morality has no other demonstrable ultimate function. (1978, p. 167)

Wilson also writes:

> The question of interest is no longer whether human social behavior is genetically determined; it is to what extent. The accumulated evidence for a large hereditary component is more detailed and compelling than most persons, including even geneticists, realize. I will go further: it already is decisive. (1978, p. 19)

But something is contradictory about Wilson's position. He writes, "Human social evolution is *obviously* more cultural and genetic" (1978, p. 153, emphasis added). He goes on to say that selfishness governs all emotions, even compassion. These views raise the following question: If the selfishness of genes is ubiquitous and dominant, how could the social dimension be more influential on human behavior? The contradiction appears vivid when Wilson discusses altruism. Like Dawkins, Wilson views altruism as ultimately self-destructive behavior on behalf of kin. Simply put, altruism is about genes, selfishness, and kinship. Credit Wilson, however, for knowing only too well that altruism—which seems counterintuitive to our selfish nature—needs a good explanation from emergent proponents of natural selection theory:

> This brings us to the central theoretical problem of sociobiology: how can altruism, which by definition reduces personal fitness, possibly evolve by natural selection? The answer is kinship: if the genes causing the altruism are shared by two organisms because of common descent, and if the altruistic act by one

organism increases the joint contribution of these genes to the next generation, the propensity to altruism will spread through the gene pool. This occurs even though the altruist makes less of a solitary contribution to the gene pool as the price of its altruistic act. (1980, p. 3)

In an essay titled, *Human Decency Is Animal*, Wilson elaborates on this explanation:

How can altruism persist? In the case of social insects, there is no doubt at all. Natural selection has been broadened to include a process called kin selection. The self-sacrificing termite soldier protects the rest of the colony, including the queen and king which are the soldier's parents. As a result, the soldier's more fertile brothers and sisters flourish, and it is they which multiply the altruistic genes that are shared with the soldier by close kinship. One's own genes are multiplied by the greater production of nephews and nieces. (1975, p. 42)

But history offers numerous examples that contest this definition of altruism. What of the altruism of John Brown, an Anglo, who fought heroically for the liberation of slaves? What about the gentiles who, at great personal cost, housed Jews during World War II? Numerous examples abound. Indeed, Wilson can point to no research that shows that kinship makes for greater acts of altruism. On the hand, history offers numerous acts of altruism that are unrelated to kinship.

In *On Human Nature*, Wilson equivocates and adds further confusion to the matter: "The altruistic impulse can be irrational and unilaterally directed at others; the bestower expresses no desire for equal return and performs no unconscious actions leading to the same end" (p. 155). If so, what becomes of the selfishness that supposedly holds human action on a short leash? From the standpoint of the theory of the natural selection, how is such random behavior possible? Other questions are raised from the notion that altruism is "relatively unaffected by social reward or punishment beyond childhood" (p. 155). Foremost, what becomes of Wilson's assertion about the superior efficacy of the cultural factor in fashioning human social evolution? Moreover, as a solid correlation supposedly exists between altruism and kinship (decreasing as kinship relationship becomes increasingly distant), what determines the self-sacrificing acts of John Brown and Harriett Tubman that obviously had nothing to do with kinship? Finally, what becomes of the social contract and the "good society?" Wilson does say that selfishness is necessary for the good society and "the nearly perfect social contract" (p. 157). He adds further to the confusion when he alludes to still another kind of altruism—soft core altruism—based exclusively on reciprocation, and which supposedly characterizes much of social behavior. The calculation at the heart of reciprocation makes deceit the hallmark of this kind of altruism. In other words, human beings act altruistically for purely selfish ends. However, even this kind altruism cannot explain the unselfishness of a John Brown or a Louise Michel. Understandably, Murray Bookchin is livid:

> What is so vexing [about Wilson's position] . . . is that human altruism, conceived as a concern for other people and the human condition generally, is by no means reducible to the underlying emotions that are considered to evolve through genes. Indeed, innumerable thinkers and many revolutionary social movements in the past were guided not by kin selection but by great ideals. . . . For profoundly cultural reasons they evoked strong passions in many idealists and produced passionate social upheavals, guided by great ideas that had no evident associated with genes or memes. Yes—human genetic equipment was involved in the *emergence* of passions, as were hormones like epinephrine. But the evolution of these passions, their sophistication, and the extent to which they powered ideas rooted in intellection were too evidently cultural to reduce to genetic influences. (1995, p. 47)

Wilson is a biological determinist. His acknowledgment of the efficacy of environment weighs far less than his belief that selfishness is the foundation of the good society. Certainly, Wilson argues credibly that environment affects behavior. Particularly noteworthy is the research by Harry F. Harlow on the effects of maternal nurturing on socialization of rhesus monkeys. In brief, Harlow found that rhesus monkeys deprived of maternal nurturing became socially dysfunctional, sexually and parentally incompetent, and had long-lasting psychological impairment. In the end, though, Wilson believes that the environment only shapes and molds, whereas the genes set the design and plan.

Wilson shows all of this plainly when the discussion turns to aggression. In *Sociobiology*, he writes: "It does not matter whether the aggression is wholly innate or is acquired partly or wholly by learning. We are now sophisticated enough to know that the capacity to learn certain behaviors is itself a genetically controlled and therefore evolved trait" (1980, p. 126). Wilson never describes the other behaviors, but obviously the suggestion is that aggression is such a behavior. Looking at behaviors that arguably fall within the family of aggression, one has to wonder whether Wilson would say that racism is such a trait? Tribalism? Heterosexism? Indeed, the pervasiveness of such behaviors would seem worthy of trait status. It is common, after all, to hear justifications of such behaviors on grounds of protecting our well-being and survival—for example, homosexuals supposedly bring AIDS and prey on our children; blacks supposedly bring down property values; Hispanics supposedly abuse governmental services; Jews supposedly hoard monetary resources; and so forth. Wilson is obviously suggesting that coercion is the only way to end racism, heterosexism, sexism, and tribalism. In *On Human Nature*, however, he makes his position abundantly clear on the question of aggression. Wilson writes:

> Are human beings innately aggressive? . . . The answer . . . is yes. Throughout history, warfare, representing only the most organized technique of aggression, has been endemic to every form of society, from hunter-gatherer bands to industrial states. During the past three centuries a majority of the countries of Europe have been engaged in war during approximately half of all the years; few have ever seen a century of continuous peace. Virtually all societies have invented elaborate sanctions against rape, extortion, and murder, while regulating their daily commerce through complex customs and laws designed to minimize the subtler but inevitable forms of conflict. Most significantly of all, the human forms of aggressive behavior are species-specific: although basically primate in form, they contain features that distinguish them from aggression in all species. (1978, p. 99)

Wilson is merely another proponent of the theory of natural selection theory who views aggression as nature. Probably the most popular proponent is Nobel laureate Konrad Lorenz. In *On Aggression*, which the *New York Times* described as "An epoch-making book . . . also a profoundly civilizing one," Lorenz argues that aggression is actually a good thing for the preservation of species: "[W]e find that aggression, far from being the diabolical, destructive principle that classical psychoanalysis makes it out to be, is really an essential part of the life-preserving organization of instincts" (1963, p. 48). Among other things, aggression makes for selection of the strongest through fighting and other contests, evolution of skills to defend young offspring, and prevents exhaustion of resources by forcing animals of the same species to find new environments and resources. No doubt, many proponents of natural selection will also contend that aggression is vital for the retribution that ensures the evolution of cooperation. In fact, Christy Turner, a prominent anthropologist at Arizona State University, who seems to be now calling for a kind of anthrobiology, speculates that human beings possess a proclivity for cannibalism. He speculates about cannibalism being an artifact of evolutionary adaptation:

> Terrorizing, mutilating, and murdering might be evolutionarily useful behaviors when directed against unrelated competitors. And what better way to amplify opponents' fear than to reduce victims to the subhuman level of cooked meat, especially when they include infants and children from whom no power or prestige could be derived but whose consumption would surely further terrorize, demean, and insult their helpless parents or community. . . . The benefits would be threefold: community control, control of reproductive behavior (that is, dominating access to women), and food. From the standpoint of sociobiology, then, cannibalism could well represent useful behavior done by well-adjusted, normal adults acting out their ultimate, evolutionarily channelled behavior. On the other hand, one can easily look upon violence and cannibalism as socially pathological. (1999, pp. 477-478)

What is remarkable about Wilson's understanding of aggression is that no research about human beings and aggression is cited as support. Instead, he continues to look at rhesus monkeys and other animals to understand human beings. Wilson writes, "A much more likely circumstance for any given aggressive species, and one that I suspect is true for man, is that the aggressive responses vary according to the situation in a genetically programmed manner" (1980, p. 127). This kind of speculation is troubling for a variety of reasons. As R. C. Lewontin, Steven Rose, and Leon Kamin, authors of *Not In Our Genes*, point out, "If aggression is manifest only in *some* environments, then in what important sense is it innate and why do we not simply avoid the wrong environments?" Lewontin and company also challenge Wilson on the supposed relationship between primates and humans:

Evolutionary biologists distinguish between homologous structures, which have been inherited from common ancestors, and
analogous structures, which may be similar in function but arise
from quite different evolutionary sources. So, the wings of birds
and bats are homologous, since they are formed from the fore-
limbs of vertebrates, while the wings of birds and insects are
only analogous . If several closely related forms all have the
same trait, it is reasonable to suppose that they have inherited it
from a recent common ancestor. However, humans have no very
close living relatives. . . . It is simply not possible to say that traits
that appear to be homologous between humans and apes are
really so. (1984, p. 255)

Wilson also never addresses the considerable research that
specifically addresses human aggression. In fact, emergent findings
derived from the actual study of human beings damn Wilson's theory of aggression the most. The research that looks at aggression and
human beings shows compellingly that environmental/social/cul-
tural/neurological factors better explain aggression. Dorothy Lewis,
a psychiatrist at New York's Bellevue Hospital and a professor at
New York University School of Medicine, and Jonathan Pincus, a
professor of neurology at Georgetown University Medical Center,
find that violent criminals are distinguishable by physical injury to
various parts of the brain—cortex and frontal lobes—that control
judgment, decision-making, and everyday organizing. Such injury
usually resulted from child abuse. A study of a group of Vietnam
veterans also found that those with similar kinds of brain injury were
significantly more violent and aggressive than veterans without such
injury (Gladwell, 1997).

Raine, Buchsbaum, and LaCasse (1997) have also found that
violent criminals tend to have relatively localized brain dysfunction
of the kind that Pincus and others (e.g., Weiger & Bear, 1988) link
empirically and conceptually to violence. In another study using subjects from Denmark, Raine and another set of researchers (1994, 1997)
found that those who suffered from both birth complications and
early maternal rejection were most likely to become violent criminals
in adulthood (at age 18). These data support other research that finds
a relationship between disruption to the mother-infant bonding
process and criminal behavior. In accounting for the contribution of
birth complications to violent behavior, Raine, Brennan, and
Mednick speculate:

It is not known precisely how birth complications predispose to violence, but it is possible that such complications result in brain dysfunction and associated neurological and neuropsychological deficits that in turn directly and indirectly predispose to violence. For example, birth complications could lead to cognitive deficits that in turn lead to school failure, occupational failure, and ultimately violence. Similarly, birth complications may contribute to neuropsychiatric deficits and lack of self-control, resulting in explosive, impulsive aggression. The effects of any such brain dysfunction may in turn be exacerbated by a negative early psychosocial environment. (1994, p. 987)

Malcolm Gladwell (1997) reports on the work by Mary Main and Carol George who found among a group of disadvantaged toddlers that those who had been physically abused usually responded to a distressed peer aggressively, whereas nonabused toddlers responded with empathy and attempts to offer comfort. This is consistent with a tremendous body of research that shows a relationship between the amount of touching that children receive and their adult social behavior. In short, touching is vital to our emotional and physical development.

Malcolm Gladwell also reports on the work by Bruce Perry who found through brain scans that neglected children suffered from permanent neurological damage as a result of insufficient affectionate nurturance. According to Perry:

There are parts of the brain that are involved in attachment behavior—the connectedness of one individual to another—and in order for that to be expressed we have to have a certain nature of experience and have that experience at the right time. If early in life you are not held and given all the somatosensory stimuli that are associated with what we call love, that part of the brain is not organized in the sane way. (quoted in Gladwell, 1997, p. 140)

Particularly noteworthy among Perry's findings is the entry of love and affection into the equation. This finding seems to point to a natural human striving for affection. By contrast, Wilson and Dawkins view love and affection as artifacts of manipulation that have evolved for purely selfish purposes. Such purposes, again, are specifically about the survival of genes. But something is noticeably amiss with Wilson and company's understanding of affection. Dawkins contends that survival machines use emotion and affection for protection against foes and the acquisition of resources and mates so as to allow for the perpetuation of genes through offspring. This explanation seems defensive until the aforementioned findings enter the equation and point to something existential. Why does deprivation of love, affection, warmth, touch, and so forth have such debilitating effects on human development? What other factors could explain the dysfunctional behaviors? The point is that deprivation of affection actually seems to lead to behaviors, such as aggression and hostility, that threaten the survival of genes by heightening the chances of violent confrontation with others. This reality is contrary to what natural selection posits about being human. It seems that the need for affection reflects something existential, that is, pointing to a meaning of life other than that of survival. This natural yearning for love and affection and the positive consequences of such on the quality of life seem to point to a natural predisposition to belong. It all seems contrary to any theory that views genes as ruthlessly selfish and always about the business of scheming others for purely selfish purposes.

The reality is that environmental/social factors function both ways. That is, such factors are equally capable of causing or preventing criminal and delinquent behavior. Numerous intervention programs have been shown to be effective in accomplishing the latter (e.g., Brooks-Gunn et al., 1993; Farrington, 1994; Johnson & Walker, 1987; Lally, Mangione, & Honig, 1988; Larson, 1980; Seitz, Rosenbaum, & Apel, 1985). Equally compelling is the research on various native peoples who have been found to be relatively nonviolent and nonaggressive (e.g., Briggs, 1970; Fry, 1992; Howell & Willis, 1989; Montagu, 1978). For instance, Gielen (1995) reports that Ladakh society, located in northwest India, is relatively nonviolent. According to Gielen:

> [W]e find in Ladakh a minimum of hostility and violence among the people, very few serious crimes, a quiet but persistent disapproval of greed, covetousness, and exploitiveness, little competition and individualism, a good deal of interpersonal trust and cooperation, a general prevalence of good humor, a relative absence of depressive moods, a fairly easy going attitude toward sex, and relatively high levels of equality between the sexes. (1995, p. 201)

Gielen believes that the nonviolent nature of Ladakh society is a result of a strong pervading Buddhist ethos that stresses good deeds, so as to gain religious merit. Examples of good deeds that make for religious merit are altruism, cooperation, detachment, serenity, honesty, compassion, and emphasis on quiet dignity.

The problem with Wilson and company's assertions about human aggression is that direct research on human behavior strongly suggests that aggression is an artifact of dysfunctionality. The problem also attends to the other notions that undergird applications of natural selection theory to human behaviors, such as selfishness, manipulation, coercion, and competition. The point is, holding the other notions coherently together without aggression is difficult. So the potential loss of aggression is crippling to the validity of applications of natural selection theory to human behavior. The emergent findings seem to have struck such a blow. Research by Perry and others strongly suggests that by simply allowing our natural strivings for affection to blossom, aggression never enters the equation, except as a result of exceptional circumstances. In this way, biological determinism atomizes human beings by undermining the relationship between community and being human. It is a point that Bookchin, too, observes:

> If one reduces society from a human phenomenon to mere aggregations of living things—not only organisms but genes and memes—culture is inconceivable. We would have a collection of living beings, but not a *society* organized into mutable institutions.
> Sociobiology, with its atomized genes and memes, patently deals with collections, aggregations, and heaps of organisms rather than with authentic societies characterized by a radically different level of association and organization of superficially discrete beings—specifically, *human* beings. Human beings exist in relationships with each other that are not defined by genes alone, if at all. In this respect, sociobiology is not *social* at all. (1995, p. 47)

The present political/social/cultural environment is responsible for the success of sociobiology. Sociobiology reinforces popular understandings of liberation. It is about autonomy. It also emerges from the spoils of competition and it represents the negation of anything that encumbers competition, such as regulations, government, and so on. Market forces are fecund. Proponents of the status quo echo the claim that competition cultivates the most proficient ways of being. Supposedly, competition makes for the fittest, smartest, strongest, and swiftest. The result is a superior society. Consequently, any undercutting of competition supposedly represents a threat to liberation.

Economics and Politics

Most of the assumptions that ground our economic and political systems originate in Charles Darwin's natural selection theory. The assumptions are captured best in game theory. Game theory is a branch of mathematics that was originally designed to deal with conflict situations (Zagare, 1984). The establishment of the theory is credited to mathematician John von Neuman and economist Oskar Morgenstern. It is John Forbes Nash Jr., however, who is responsible for the popularity of game theory. He received a Nobel Prize for his contributions. Key to Nash's contribution is the notion that human beings are motivated by self-interest. Sylvia Nasar writes, "Nash tended to think of people as out of touch with one another and acting on their own. He had grown up in a town in the southern Appalachians where fortunes were made from the roaring, raw businesses of rails, coal, scrap metal, and electric power. Self-interest, not common agreement on some collective good, seemed sufficient to create a tolerable order" (1998, p. 226). Game theory has been extensively used to study the processes of decision making or choice making, and goal competition and cooperation. Its mathematical foundation, proponents contend, affords better empirical tests, greater applicability, specificity and objectivity, and superior prediction of factual occurrences (Bostrom, 1968). In sum, game theory mathematicizes the study of human behavior, and for many economists and political scientists, this a good thing. It reinforces the assumption that human beings are as predictable and manipulable as so many other aspects of this world. It celebrates the power of man to use his rational faculty to unlock all the secrets of world. It reinforces the belief that *man*, relying on his rational faculty, can gain dominion over the world. In sum, game theory is born of a belief that this is a world without mystery.

Game theory deals with rationally constructed and conducted conflicts between players. Each player pursues well-defined interests and chooses between at least two alternative courses of action. In relation to conflict situations, Steinfatt and Miller explain:

> Game theory is concerned with how to win a game, with strategies of move sequences that maximize the player's chance to gain and minimize his chance for loss. Because a major ingredient in conflict situations is the desire to gain something one does not possess and to hold onto that which one does possess, certain games are analogous to particular conflict situations and game theory serves as a model to predict the behavior of a person in such conflict situations attempting to gain those ends. (1974, p. 38)

A game consists of a series of moves by a player aimed at attaining maximum gain or minimum loss. The underlying premise in game theory is that players will act rationally. In other words, each player would act to attain the most preferred outcomes, given the constraint that the other players are also acting similarly. Many scholars classify game theory as a kind of normative theory, that is, a theory of how human beings should act. However, Zagare argues that game theory has the capacity to be a rigorous descriptive theory: "Once some of its key assumptions are operationalized and ascribed empirical meaning, game theory can also be considered a descriptive, or positive theory, capable of explanation and prediction" (1984, p. 8). He also contends that the theory has the capability to develop into a fully rigorous, deductive theory of human behavior that could become "a unifying force in the social sciences, encompassing economics, psychology, politics, and history within a single mathematical theory."

The most commonly used gaming situation in game theory research is the Prisoner's Dilemma (PD). In fact, this is precisely the gaming situation that most proponents of natural selection theory employ. This is also the research protocol that Axelrod used. In a PD game, each of two players has two choices, a cooperative choice and a competitive choice. PD is a simulation where two players are apprehended by police and then separated. After being separated, each must choose whether to confess or remain silent. Remaining silent represents a cooperative choice (cooperating with the other player). If both players remain silent (both cooperative), they will be held in jail for a few days until police must drop the case and release them (minimum gain for both players). If they both confess (both competitive), they will both be sent to prison for relatively short sentences (minimum loss for both players). If, however, one remains silent (cooperative) and the other confesses (competitive), the silent prisoner will be sent to prison for a long sentence (maximum loss), and the one who confesses will be freed immediately (maximum gain).

Early research shows that approximately 60 to 80 percent of the choices with PD gaming were competitive. This finding would seem to confirm all that proponents of natural selection theory purport about selfishness and competition. Beisecker (1970) is of the opinion that each participant would prefer to act in a manner which yields him or her even greater reward, "But he realized that he cannot because he cannot obtain the cooperation of the other" (p. 110). Consequently, mutual cooperation is really a compromise, a less desirable option, so as to obtain at least something from the situation. Beisecker's argument parallels that of Dawkins and others. He believes that selfishness is at the root of all human behavior and that cooperation emerges only when there are no better options for selfish gain. However, emergent research on game theory raises serious doubts about this conclusion. This research interrogates fundamental assumptions that undergird extant game theory modeling.

Game theory assumes that rationality is about selfishness and competition. However, research by Cox, Lobel, and McLeod (1991) suggests that this is a narrow and decidedly European view of rationality. Cox et al. used PD to assess ethnic group differences in cooperative and competitive behaviors among Asians, blacks, Hispanics, and Anglos. Their findings revealed that Asians, blacks, and Hispanics had a cooperative orientation to a task, whereas Anglos had a competitive orientation. Moreover, groups composed of Asians, blacks, Hispanics, and Anglos acted more cooperatively than all-Anglo groups, and those behavioral differences tended to increase when the situation cues favored cooperation. Further, Anglos were the only group to become more competitive when they expected cooperation from the other player.

These findings suggest that Asians, blacks, and Hispanics are more likely than Anglos to view the objective of the game in cooperative rather than competitive terms. This observation is consistent with other research using variations of PD that found that cooperatively oriented subjects responded in kind to a competitive strategy, but quickly reverted to cooperative behavior in response to a cooperative strategy, even though the payoff matrix advantaged responding competitively. On the other hand, competitively oriented players displayed competitive behavior under both conditions. The point is that rationality is culturally derived. In other words, what makes for the best decision is contextual and relational. This by no means suggest that our underlying decision-making processes are purely social constructions. What constitutes conflict, how conflict is dealt with, and what outcomes mean are social constructions. In short, conflict is relational, transactional, and cultural. It is neither universal nor constant.

The point here is that game theory wrongly assumes that conflict is fixed. To posit that conflict is negative or to understand conflict negatively represents only a certain meaning—actually a narrow view—of conflict. As with any other social construction, conflict is susceptible to a variety of different meanings, and each meaning can bring forth a different way of dealing with conflict. Accordingly, meaning mediates both our understanding and our approach to conflict, and the way that conflict is understood recursively determines our predisposition to such a situation. Cox and company show this plainly. Asians, blacks, and Hispanics saw cooperation rather than competition as the best decision. In contrast, Anglos saw competition as the best decision. Consequently, Beisecker is wrong to claim sweepingly that cooperation represents an undesirable behavior. This position is culturally biased.

Game theory also assumes that players acting rationally would seek maximum gain or minimum loss. Steinfatt and Miller posit this explicitly: "[A] major ingredient in conflict situations is the desire to gain something one does not possess and to hold onto that which one does possess" (1974, p. 38). Thus, acting selfishly and competitively would be normative. In other words, from a rational standpoint, the best decision is to act competitively, as this ensures either maximum gain or minimum loss. If my opponent acts cooperatively, I stand to gain the most; on the other hand, let us say that my opponent acts competitively—this still only minimizes my losses. Dawkins contends that when each player recognizes that the other player would act competitively, resulting in short prison terms for both players (minimum loss for each), this would lead to the evolution of cooperation. But by presupposing that human beings are both selfish and rational, Dawkins and company are committed to viewing conflict confrontationally, as about maximizing gains or minimizing losses. Conflict becomes synonymous with competition and selfishness. Competition and selfishness even undergird the evolution of cooperation. In fact, Beisecker (1970) argues that the notion of cooperation is foreign to the theory of games. If cooperation does appear, Beisecker contends, selfishness is the underlying motivation. Inadvertently, however, Robert Axelrod's findings contradict this reasoning.

Axelrod found through a series of PD tournaments that a strategy based on cooperation (TIT FOR TAT) was the most successful. This strategy is based on reciprocity. He writes:

> TIT FOR TAT's robust success is due to being nice, provocable, forgiving, and clear. Its niceness means that it is never the first to defect [act competitively], and this property prevents it from getting into unnecessary trouble. Its retaliation discourages the other side from persisting whenever defection is tried. Its forgiveness helps restore mutual cooperation. And its clarity makes its behavioral pattern easy to recognize; and once recognized, it is easy to perceive that the best way of dealing with TIT FOR TAT is to cooperate with it. (1984, p. 176)

Economists and political scientists constantly highlight Axelrod's research. It is seen as confirming applications of natural selection theory to human behavior. However, the most vociferous proponents of Axelrod's research are proponents of market forces. His research is seen as showing that human beings act best when rational, that selfishness can be harnessed for the good of all, and that morality is best when derived organically, that is, without government regulation. In short, Axelrod's findings supposedly show the disciplining capability of market forces. Besides the validation that natural selection theory seems to lend to Axelrod's thesis, what also helps is the mathematization of human behavior that game theory modeling supposedly affords (shown in the numerous mathematical models and equations that are constantly referred to—an appendix is aptly titled "Proofs of the Theoretical Propositions").

Proponents now claim that market forces have a natural disciplining mechanism that is conducive to protecting and harnessing our *differences* for the good of all. Supposedly, market forces best match rewards with talents. Hence, there is no justification for the many—who end up with few of the spoils—to envy the few (the cognitive elites) who end up with most of the spoils of market exchanges. The few are simply deserving, proponents of market forces contend. This is the way of the world. Indeed, proponents contend that market forces should be celebrated for allowing our supposed natural differences to make for the evolution of a natural and fair hierarchical ordering. Supposedly, such an ordering is vital to the ordering of human beings so as to stop the onset of social devolution and chaos. Moreover, proponents contend that market forces offer us a nonviolent outlet for safe and productive channeling of our aggressive and destructive instincts.

Advocates of the unleashing of market forces also contend that the end of government will also bring the end of deviant and delinquent behaviors that now seem so uneradicable. This will be a natural consequence of market forces consistently punishing rather than encouraging such behavior. Attending to the weak, especially as this tends to demand empathy, unselfishness, and cooperation, only undercuts the good society. Proponents contend that anything that runs against the calculus of natural selection only prolongs the misery of the weak and fosters destructive habits among the strongest, brightest, and fittest—habits that will eventually encumber social evolution. In fact, Dawkins reasons thusly, though he argues for the bridling of selfishness. Consequently, many authors and legislators now demand the unleashing of market forces and the devolution of government. Capitalism is cast as the only system consistent with the objective truths of the world. It demands that human beings act rationally, thus affording prediction and control, elements that are supposedly vital for any good society. Capitalism exploits our selfishness for collective gain and harnesses the supposedly evolutionary virtues of competition.

But a reread of Axelrod's findings supports a different conclusion. A strategy that leads with cooperation seems to contradict the ruthless selfishness that is at the root of applications of natural selection theory to human behavior. Regardless of whether this is the best strategy for the evolution of cooperation, such a position makes those using such a strategy overly vulnerable, which seems to be the antithesis of ruthless selfishness. Yet, according to Axelrod, this strategy is supposedly robust enough to work without any kind of trust, friendship, and familiarity with the opposing player. In fact, according to Axelrod, being rational is even unnecessary. The best strategy also stresses clarity. In other words, the best strategy demands being vulnerable and transparent. Dawkins, however, contends that exploitive deceit is the hallmark of human behavior. He also claims that human beings' emotive faculty has evolved purely for such purposes. If so, how does Dawkins explain Axelrod's finding that being nice, open and vulnerable characterized the most successful strategy?

Axelrod misses the fact that decision-making occurs within a relational, transformational, and existential context. He even believes that leaving out communication and relationship is a plus:

> The value of an analysis without them [relational history and verbal communication] is that it can help to clarify some of the subtle features of the interaction—features which might otherwise be lost in the maze of complexities of the highly particular circumstances in which choice must actually be made. It is the very complexity of reality which makes the analysis of an abstract interaction so helpful as an aid to understanding. (1984, p. 19)

In other words, Axelrod believes that the complexity that characterizes decision-making has no real bearing on the process. He believes that a fixed set of configurations undergird our decision-making processes and he seeks to uncover them. This is the objective of reductionism. It is the complexity of our *beingness*, however, that constitutes decision-making. This complexity entails the hopes, beliefs, assumptions, aspirations, and fears that shape decision-making. Complexity reflects the negotiation of self. In attempting to strip away all complexity, self is lost. Axelrod atomizes human beings. He gives the self no opportunity to bear on being human. The result is that nothing is learned about how human beings transact self through conflict, negotiation, and decision-making.

Axelrod believes that being nice, open, and vulnerable merely represent the most rational strategy. It is the only strategy that assures survival by thwarting the escalation of conflict that deceit and deception engender. However, besides thwarting the escalation of conflict, this strategy also undermines hierarchy. Transparency blocks manipulation. Deception and manipulation foster subordination by suppressing the open expression of conflict and diversity. Accordingly, hierarchy springs from dysfunctional communication, that is, communication laden with deceit, deception, distrust, and suspicion. It is an artifact of deception. The evolution of being nice, open, and vulnerable represents the natural striving for human relations devoid of manipulation, domination, and subordination. In short, Axelrod's research suggests that human beings possess both the means and desires to end hierarchy.

Noticeably absent from PD is any communication between players. The omission is understandable. Game theory, after all, is predicated on the view that human beings and conflict are controlled by nature. However, after a review of numerous studies, Steinfatt and Miller (1974) found that communication between players correlates with cooperative moves and mutually beneficial outcomes. It was also found that communication mediates aggression. Such findings compellingly show that communication is central to any understanding of conflict. However, the quantification that game theory exponents demand obstructs any serious consideration of communication. Quantification strips away the complexity that constitutes communication. It obliterates the relational dynamics that fashion the creation of meaning. The result is that communication is reduced to the transaction of messages. In this way, exponents of game theory misunderstand the crux of communication: the evolution and negotiation of meaning. According to Dennis Davis and James Jasinki:

> The most basic and common function of communication is performance, not transmission of information. Performance occurs in rituals and other practices used within communities to coordinate experience and induce common perceptions of the social world. Performance practices serve to sustain culture through structuring of experience, not through transmission and learning of discrete bits of information. . . . It promotes feeling with or involvement in, not knowledge of, the social world. (1993, p. 144)

Communication is a complex phenomenon. As Austin Babrow (1993) observes, "Communication involves multiple, substantively distinct processes; these processes may be redundant, complementary, or contradictory; and processes may mediate or moderate other processes" (p. 110). Viewing communication as transmission fosters the belief that humans are without self. Human beings are simply the most evolved life forms—merely distinguishable by our ability to transmit memes. Consequently, proponents of Charles Darwin's natural selection theory give us no schemes to look at the construction of self. Game theory is about the behavior of our supposedly different natures. It is self, however, that distinguishes human beings from animals. What communication manifests and transforms is self. Self is what makes the distinction between meaning and information. This distinction, as Alan Wolfe points out, is significant:

> Meaning . . . is a macrophenomenon that involves making larger sense out of smaller bits, while information reduces larger complexity into smaller, and presumably more manageable, units. Information communicates through signs; meaning through symbols. For those who seek information, context is only noise; for those concerned with meaning, context is everything. Information and meaning, in short, work at cross-purposes. (1993, p. 118)

Consequently, reductionism undermines the study of meaning, sustains erroneous and overly narrow conceptualizations of communication, and, ultimately, distorts what being human means.

Exponents of game theory, though now recognizing the need to consider communication seriously, contend that the problem is at the practical rather than the theoretical level. This stance reveals that game theorists have yet to understand fully the enormous complexity of communication. Much of the fault rests with the ethos of mathematization that undergirds much extant theorizing about the human condition. The mathematization of social behavior, the hallmark of which is game theory, bespeaks the profound level of reductionism. Mathematization is a form of reductionism, and reductionism undermines any meaningful understanding of human behavior. As Nicotera and Rodriguez point out:

> [T]he problem of mathematization is the root of the downfall of game theory in the study of communication and conflict. If com-

munication is conceptualized simply as information exchange, the problem is simplified. If, however, communication is seen as a host of relational variables, factors of interdependency, and cultural rules and values, then game theory cannot account for it. Such things cannot be consistently mathematized. Game theory relies on binary decision points; human interaction is infinitely more complex. This is not to argue that human interaction is inherently immeasurable, but that game theory assumptions rely on too simple a measurement. Game theory relies on a constant value for this variable, and human interaction is continually in flux. (1994, p. 15)

Many proponents of natural selection theory consider charges of vulgar reductionism a cheap shot. Daniel Dennett calls for a distinction between *good* and *greedy* reductionism and *uncompromising* and *compromising* reductionism. He argues, "There is no reason to be compromising about what I call good reductionism. It is simply the commitment to non-question-begging science without any cheating by embracing mysteries [!] or miracles [!] at the outset" (1995, p. 82). Dennett believes that without reductionism humanity will resort to mysticism to understand the world. Accordingly, reductionism is supposedly vital to the making of the good society.

Dennett evidently believes that the world is without mystery. He also believes that rationality can unlock all the secrets of the world. He writes, "It must be true that there is an evolutionary explanation of how our memes and genes interacted to create the policies of human cooperation that we enjoy in civilization—we haven't figured out all the details yet, but it must be true unless there are skyhooks in the offering . . ." (p. 470). He believes that the world behaves rationally. His equation posits that rational beings, using rational means to study a rationally organized world, can find rational truths. E. O. Wilson (1998) contends similarly, "All tangible phenomena from the birth of stars to the workings of social institutions are based on material processes that are ultimately reducible, however long and torturous, to the laws of physics." Naturally, Dennett also sees culture as a rational phenomenon. He writes, "What this reflection makes vivid is the fact that what is preserved and transmitted in cultural evolution is informational—in a media-neutral, language-neutral sense" (1995, pp. 353-354). In short, culture is about messages. It is reducible.

Dennett posits a representational view of culture. He believes that human beings can potentially exist outside of culture. In reality,

however, cultures are ontological rather than merely representational. Cultures exist within us and through us. Cultures represent the
co-construction of situated meanings. As Lee Thayer observes:

> A culture, therefore, is comprised of all of those means by which
> we mystify ourselves. Mind, therefore, is something more than
> merely internalized culture, and culture is something more than
> merely externalized mind. That something more is that they are
> the same thing, and the trick of language, of communication, is
> to make them appear to us to be separate things, so that we can
> pretend to an innocence long lost to us, in the same way that the
> trick of language, of communication, is to make the knower and
> the known appear to us to be separate things, so that we can pre-
> tend to be innocent of both. (1997, p. 8)

Coercion is subtly legitimized when self is presumably
nonexistent. The belief is reinforced that humans possess the propensity to act as do other animals. Coercion is still significant to the making of the good society. In this way, Axelrod attempts—despite his
findings—to legitimize our deep distrust and suspicion of our
humanity. He reinforces the belief that coercion is vital for the good
society. In end, however, Axelrod and other proponents of natural
selection theory make no compelling argument about hierarchy and
coercion being vital for the making of the good society.

Sociosexology

Proponents of natural selection theory view gender relations as cen-
tering around coercion and manipulation. It is about males trying to
have as many offsprings as possible with as many females so as to
ensure the survival and well-being of the largest amount of their
(males') genes. In turn, females only copulate with those males who
can be coercively enticed to stay after the offsprings are born in order
to help with nurturance and protection to ensure the survival and
well-being of the largest amount of their (females') genes. In short,
males constantly coerce females to have sex, and females constantly
try to entrap males to stay after sex. The selfish nature of both genes
and the conflicting interest make coercion a fundamental element of
human relations. In *The Evolution of Human Sexuality*, Donald Symons
(1990) posits this argument. Sociobiologists have hailed his contribution to our understanding of human sexuality and gender relations
as ground-breaking.

Yet Symons is working with many tenuous assumptions. He assumes that the chances of gene continuity for males increases through promiscuous mating rather than staying and helping a particular female raise healthy and productive offspring. For human beings, this assumption is contrary to all findings about child development. Simply put, both parents matter. The self-interest of the males involves staying and helping with the nurturing process. Moreover, according to sociobiologists, new males who mate with females after the other males have mated and disappeared tend to kill off the offspring of other males so as to favor their own (the new) offspring. So, what is really the worth to males of abandoning mating partners and offspring? Further, efforts to find new mates increase the probability of contests between males that can potentially decrease their chances of survival. In *The Use and Abuse of Biology: An Anthropological Critique of Sociobiology*, Marshall Sahlins, Professor of Anthropology at the University of Chicago, writes:

> The major inadequacy ensues from . . . [the] neglect to figure into the calculus the increased mortality chances among males [for] scarce female resources, and correspondingly intense competition among promiscuous males. There is no showing . . . that the reproductive advantages of desertion for the male are any greater than fitness losses he is liable to incur in competition— not to mention that abandonment of his one-time consort reduces her chances of raising his offspring. Without additional assumptions or observations, there is no basis at all for supposing that this kind of exploitation of females maximizes the individual male's reproduction. (1976, p. 90)

Other scholars posit a relation between gender and domination. In *Why Men Rule: A Theory of Male Dominance*, Steven Goldberg, Chairman of the Department of Sociology at City College, City University of New York, argues that patriarchy is a product of nature rather than nurture. Drawing upon the research of biochemists, biologists, endocrinologists, and psychologists, Goldberg argues that the universality of patriarchy (male attainment and male dominance) results from neuroendocrinological differences between men and women:

> The neuro-endocrinological differences are such that the presence of hierarchy (any hierarchy), high-status role, or member of the other sex elicits from the male, more readily, more often, and

more strongly than from the female: 1. emotions of "competitive-
ness," the tendency—the impulse—for attainment and dominance (whether this tendency, this impulse, is termed a "need"
or a "drive"); 2. relative suppression of other emotions and
needs and a sacrifice of rewards (health, family, relaxation, and
so forth) that compete with the need for attainment and dominance; 3. actions required for attainment of position, status, and
dominance. (1993, pp. 64-65)

Many anthropologists contend that Goldberg is correct.
Margaret Mead, who is arguably one of the foremost anthropologists
of this century, writes that Goldberg's thesis is, "persuasive and accurate. It is true, as Professor Goldberg points out, that all the claims so
glibly made for societies ruled by women are nonsense. We have no
reason to believe that they ever existed . . . men everywhere have
been the leaders in public affairs and the final authorities at home."
However, Charlene Spretnak (1991), author of *States of Grace*, contends that matriarchy—or what she calls matrifocal, matristic, matri-
centric, gynecentric—is really the negation of patriarchy rather than
merely an hierarchy with women at the top. In short, women have a
different conception of power from that of men. As regards the historical record, Spretnak contends:

[M]any matrifocal, matrilineal cultures were pressured to shift to
patriarchal arrangements when they were confronted with the
dominant forces of Christianity, Islam, or Eurocentric colonial-
ism. Male-dominant cultures certainly existed before those powerful forces of social, economic, and religious conversion . . .
spread out over the world, but they did account for a sizable
boost in the incidence of patriarchal societies. (1991, p. 130)

Goldberg posits that he is neither advocating, justifying, nor
defending discrimination against women. His aim, he claims, is simply to explain the universality of patriarchy. He writes:

[U]niversality does not *demonstrate* inevitability any more than
the fact that the sun has appeared every morning for billions of
years *demonstrates* that it will appear tomorrow. . . . Inevitability
is not a deduction from universality (which is necessary, but not
sufficient, for inevitability); it is the hypothetical mechanism sug-
gested by universality that renders likely the inevitability, once
that hypothetical mechanism has been examined and corroborat-
ed. (p. 179)

But a glaring problem with Goldberg's argument is the omission of communication. He assumes that gender differences naturally make for hierarchy. However, the fact that the natures of men and women are probably different (and let us say so only for purposes of argument) has no bearing on what those differences mean. Meaning is a relational phenomenon. It is relationships rather than natures that have meaning, so what our natures mean is relational. Accordingly, Goldberg errs by casting the argument dichotomously between domination and subordination. As Murray Bookchin so aptly points out, "A hierarchy [as well as patriarchy] is based on domination by institutionalized strata, such as gerontocracies, patriarchies, warrior modalities, shamanistic guilds, priestly corporations, and the like over subjugated strata who are visibly underprivileged on an ongoing basis" (1995, p. 49). Pierre Clastres offers many examples among native tribes throughout the western hemisphere in which hierarchical arrangements exist but coercion is nonexistent. In *Society Against The State*, he writes, "One is confronted, then, by a vast constellation of societies in which the holders of what elsewhere would be called power are actually without power, where the political is determined as a domain beyond coercion and violence, beyond hierarchical subordination; where, in a word, no relationship of command-obedience is in force" (1989, pp. 11-12). In sum, the natures of men and women, however different, have nothing to do with the legitimacy of domination, subordination, and coercion.

Psychobiology

Many of the dominant schools of thought within psychology posit an explicit distrust of the human condition. Theses abound as to why coercion is necessary for the making of the good society. Sigmund Freud, whose doctrines have enormously shaped the field, declared that "every individual is virtually an enemy of civilization, though civilization is supposed to be an object of universal human interest. . . . Thus civilization has to be defended against the individual, and its regulations, institutions and commands are directed at this task" (Freud, 1961, p. 6). He also declared that "every society must be built up on coercion and renunciation of instinct [such as incest, cannibalism, and lust for killing]. . . . One has . . . to reckon with the fact that there are present in all men destructive, and . . . anti-social and anti-cultural [instincts] (p. 7). Freud also saw most human beings as innately evil and destructive:

It is just as impossible to do without control of the masses by a minority as it is to dispense with coercion in the work of civilization. For masses are lazy and unintelligent; they have no love for instinctual renunciation, and they are not to be convinced by argument of its inevitability; and the individuals composing them support one another in giving free rein to their indiscipline. It is only through the influence of individuals who can set an example and whom [the] masses recognize as their leaders that they can be induced to perform the work and undergo the renunciations on which the existence of civilization depends. (1961, pp. 7-8)

Freud also believed that human beings are driven to satisfy instinctual—sexual—impulses. Much of what passes for civil behavior are attempts to mask (and restrain) such impulses. Freud believed that the suppression of our instinctual impulses brings misery and mental sickness. Consequently, while society needs coercion to protect its citizens from one another's instinctual impulses, society is also disease-inducing. Consequently, Freud speculated that probably primitive man was better off because he had no restrictions on his impulses.

Robert Wright, author of *The Moral Animal*, observes:

What is best in Freud is his sensing the paradox of being a highly social animal: being at our core libidinous, rapacious, and generally selfish, yet having to live civilly with other human beings— having to reach our animal goals via a tortuous path of cooperation, compromise, and restraint. From this insight flows Freud's most basic idea about the mind: it is a place of conflict between animal impulses and social reality. (1994, p. 321)

Our supposed animality makes for a natural union between the psychology of Freud and applications of natural selection theory to human behavior. The new field of study is *evolutionary psychology* or *psychobiology*. It is a psychology that corrects, according to proponents, for Freud's misconceptions of natural selection theory. Robert Wright's *The Moral Animal* offers the most popular exposition of this new field. Referring to Freud, Wright writes, "Anyone who sees humans as animals, driven by sexual and other coarse impulses, can't be all that bad" (1994, p. 315). Wright claims that many proponents of natural selection theory are simply afraid to explicate all of the supposed truths of the theory. Thus, whereas Dawkins, Wilson, and other sociobiologists are arguably reticent on a few things, Wright says that he has no such apprehensions. He believes that there is a moral responsibility to tell the truth. Accordingly, his book is laden with many strident claims that, according to him, make even others in the field flinch. The following represents a few of the claims:

> Can a Darwinian understanding of human nature help people reach their goals in life? Indeed, can it help them choose their goals in life? Can it help distinguish between practical and impractical goals? More profoundly, can it help in deciding which goals are worthy? That is, does knowing evolution has shaped our basic moral impulses help us decide which we should consider legitimate?
>
> The answers, in my opinion, are: yes, yes, yes, yes, and, finally, yes. (p. 10)
>
> . . . . Affection is a tool of hostility. We form bonds to deepen fissures. (p. 314)
>
> . . . . But many of our impulses are, by design, very strong, so any force that is to stifle them may have to be pretty harsh. It is grossly misleading to talk as if self-restraint is as easy as punching a channel on the remote control. . . .
>
> But surely it's true that the roots of all evil can be seen in natural selection, and are expressed (along with much that is good) in human nature. The enemy of justice and decency does indeed lie in our genes. (p. 151)

A book chosen by *The New York Times Book Review* as one of the best of the year—"Fiercely intelligent . . . engrossingly original . . . a feast of great thinking and writing about the most profound issues there are"—surely deserves a critical eye. But as Wright's underlying thesis rests on an application of natural selection theory to human behavior, my previous criticisms apply here as well. Despite the aforementioned problems with these sorts of appropriations of evolutionary theory, books like Wright's are becoming increasingly popular and gaining the most positive of reviews. A recent example is *Born That Way* by William Wright (1998), who, like Robert Wright, is also a journalist. William Wright also sees a conspiracy within the academy to suppress the truth about the nature of human beings. He writes that "Self-delusion on this ugly element of our species' basic equipment seems too widespread, it suggests millions of interpreters working full time to conceal the nasty truth about our homicidal leanings"

(1998, p. 269). Wright believes that our inborn inclinations make for the sexism, racism, ethnocentrism, tribalism, and other such behaviors that mark modern society. He writes:

> If there is a genetic mechanism that makes us prone to identify with one group and hostile to another, it appears to be closely related, may in fact activate, a genetic mechanism for aggression. The same neurological parlay that converts normal humans into lynch parties and murderous mobs may be more benignly at work in nursery schools and fraternity houses. Whatever the premise for group identity, it doesn't take long for the out-group to go from being different to being inferior, unworthy, evil, contemptible—until they are seen as needing harassment, punishment, retribution, perhaps annihilation. (p. 270)

The point is that psychology today resonates with the distrust of human beings that Freud articulated decades ago. In fact, this assumption is becoming increasingly explicit. In *The Perversion of Autonomy: The Proper Uses of Coercion and Constraints in a Liberal Society*, Willard Gaylin , Clinical Professor of Psychiatry at Columbia University, and Bruce Jennings, Director of The Hastings Center, contend:

> Conduct is always determined by a balance between the limited conscience of an individual and his [sic] selfish passions. This being the case, even with the best of people a certain amount of persuasion and coercion is necessary to ensure a socially acceptable environment. We must recognize that most human beings are more likely to respond to emotional forces—intimidation, compulsion, coercion, shame, pride, threat, or reward—than to appeals to reason. (1996, p. 126)

The primary tasks, according to Gaylin and Jennings, are convincing society that social control and coercion are necessary, and outlining the moral and ethical forms of social control and coercion:

> Social order is too important to human beings to do without; nature does not provide it for us by instinct, and it cannot emerge in a purely voluntary or spontaneous way, like the invisible hand of the market. Therefore, social order must be maintained on the basis of some degree of social control and coercion. The only real question is what kind of coercion it will be and on what psychological foundation it will rest. (1996, p. 185)

Gaylin and Jennings also posit that the ethos of autonomy thwarts our understanding of liberation. Any definition of liberation that is devoid of social control and coercion is a fantasy. Further, autonomy demands rationality, and as human beings mostly respond to nonrational motives, social control and coercion are necessary. Gaylin and Jennings put the matter this way:

> We are not as free and self-determining as we would like to believe, and we are not as independent as we pretend to be. We must face the fact that we are not as rational as we would like to think we are. The rational roots of our conduct are pathetically overvalued. We must appreciate the power of emotions over human behavior in order to effectively institute changes in that behavior. Despite a preference in the culture of autonomy for rational persuasion and a bias against manipulation and coercion, persuasion rarely works. It is coercion on which society must depend. (p. 126)

This conclusion raises a few concerns. As all human beings supposedly possess selfish passions and are at the whim of nonrational motives, who deserves the authority to exercise social control and coercion upon others? Gaylin and Jennings also posit that consideration of the social good should be the guiding framework. But what is the origin of this social good? Again, who has the authority to determine this good? Further, the tying of liberation with rationality is unnecessary. It is fair to say that human beings will never attain a condition of perfect rationality. In fact, as Gaylin and Jennings point out, this is actually a good thing for the survival and well-being of human beings. Human behavior is complex and multifaceted. Indeed, human motives are spiritual, biological, social, psychological, sensual, and rational. In this way, the lack of perfect rationality could be better seen as an asset rather than a shortcoming that will somehow lead human beings down the path to self-destruction. It is then unclear why Gaylin and Jennings view rationality as vital to liberation.

Gaylin and Jennings' attempt to set social control, coercion, and evolution against autonomy, liberation, and devolution also raises serious concerns. What is most disturbing is the tying of liberation to autonomy. As Gaylin and Jennings well know, any attempt to obtain full autonomy undermines the social frameworks and processes that afford the construction of our humanity. Consequently, how did autonomy come to mean liberation? It seems that Gaylin and Jennings' use of autonomy is a red herring.

Human beings are complex and multifaceted. Attempting to reduce our humanity to a dichotomy of rationality and sensuality reveals the mining of human relations for linear and causal relationships—the decoupling of complex relationships so as to find dominant motives. Yet this is exactly what Gaylin and Jennings attempt to do. The result is that the relation between human beings and community is undercut. Agency is also undercut. In addition, the status quo goes uninterrogated. It avoids any recognition of culpability or responsibility for promoting dysfunctional behavior. Consequently, Gaylin and Jennings reduce deviancy to a set of destructive human drives. All of this is seen well when they condemn graffitists as deviants:

> The romanticizing of graffiti as art by . . . an indulgent liberal community is baffling and may even be dangerous. It legitimates a clear violation of and contempt for community. The graffitist is simply expressing that which he [sic] has been taught. What is the rationale of his defenders? Graffiti is an act of narcissistic defiance; a sign of contempt for the common space. Urinating and defecating on the public streets are its logical extensions. (p. 121)

This kind of criticism comes directly out of the bowels of Freudian psychology. It is also a popular criticism of graffitists (e.g., Gadpaille, 1971; Lomas, 1976; Nierenberg, 1983). Alan Dundes (1966), of the University of Chicago, claims that the psychological motivation for writing on the wall is related to an infantile desire to play with feces: "The fact that much of the content of latrinalia does refer to defecation and urination would tend to support the assertion that there is some relationship between the acts of writing on walls and playing with feces" (p. 101). Dundes (1966) also contends that the act of defecation is the male analog of childbirth, and the writing on the wall while defecating becomes, by association, a kind of permanent substitute for the creation of a child. This explanation rests on the theory that men are envious of women's ability to bear children, and as a result they seek to find various substitute gratifications.

Lomas (1976) also believes that writing on the wall represents destructive desires. The wall symbolically represents separation. The scenario is as follows: The need-satisfying mother leaves the child helpless. The child's rage is deflected onto the wall that separates them. It is an act of revenge calculated to place the mother in a similar state of anguished helplessness. Lomas also sees writing on the wall as another way that men attempt to deal with the Oedipus complex (son's jealousy of father having sex with mother). Consequently,

Gaylin and Jennings side with those who contend that graffiti are artifacts of the less talented of society (Abel & Buckley, 1977); are a low-level expression of thwarted human interests (Opler, 1974); and that a low level of maturity is a prerequisite for graffiti indulgence (Klein, 1974). Such views, however, are now dismissed.

Many now contend that graffiti deserve attention and serious study (e.g., Boyd, 1981; Durmuller, 1986, 1988; Jones-Baker, 1981; Kohl, 1972; La Barre, 1979; Longnecker, 1977). There is at least general agreement that graffiti contain profound social, psychological, and cultural data about persons and various groups. It is also believed that graffiti satisfy a need to escape to a world of fantasy (Bonuso, 1976); that graffiti allow people to achieve a semblance of immortality (Spann, 1973); that graffiti constitute a product of the adolescent personality and are motivated by subconscious urges, impulses, and conflicts (Melhorn & Romig, 1985); and that people who produce graffiti are visually oriented and use graffiti to negotiate developmental issues (Feiner & Klein, 1982). Rodriguez and Clair (1999) contend that graffiti reveal how relations of power are being contested, what issues are worthy of being contested, and with which groups graffitists align themselves.

People also use graffiti to share their thoughts and feelings, to mark their social and cultural identity, and to define their social relationships (Durmuller, 1986). In addition, writing graffiti may release suppressed thoughts and frustrations (Gilmar & Brown, 1983). Graffiti potentially indicate attitudes, behavioral dispositions, and social processes in environments where direct measurement is problematic (Ley & Cybriwsky, 1974). It is also believed that graffiti offer an accurate index of the political temper of the times (Deiulio, 1978). According to Gumpert (1975) and Reisner and Wechsler (1974), graffiti exist because other means of self-expression are barred. Vervort and Lievens (1989) concluded that such graffiti reflect contemporary problems and reveal other elusive aspects of society. In addition, Hastings (1984) and Misic (1990) found that European soccer fans use graffiti and other symbols for identification, communication, integration, and other social rituals.

Reisner and Wechsler (1974) and Newall (1986-1987) contend that graffiti function to vent hostilities, express fantasies, communicate triumphs, declare rebellion, and promote propaganda. Likewise, Luna (1987) contends that graffiti serve as a means of communication among homeless youth to declare their identities, relationships, and communities. Brown (1978) writes: "This [graffiti] is not so much, as many would believe, the result of a desire to deface property; rather graffiti are a vehicle to communicate a message that is understood by the gangs" (p. 46). Gonzales (1994) reports on how gangs, family members, and friends in the Bronx, New York, use graffiti to honor and remember their dead. In sum, graffiti offer valuable insight to the concerns, conflicts, and other discursive behaviors of various members of society. The fact that society cannot sanction and control the content and accessibility of the discourses that appear on walls are what make graffiti a valuable communication opportunity for disenfranchised and marginalized groups.

But what most refutes Gaylin and Jennings' claims are the graffiti found in women's bathrooms. A consistent finding is that women frequently use bathroom walls for counsel and community, to exchange experiences and concerns, and seek and offer advice (e.g., Alexander, 1978; Bruner & Kelso, 1980; Reich et al., 1977). Several scholars (Bruner & Kelso, 1980; Cole, 1991; Hentschel, 1987) posit that women use the bathrooms to build a community without the aggressive and hostile features that patriarchy fosters. According to Bruner and Kelso:

> We . . . see women's inscriptions as a separate universe of discourse, one that uses their own cultural code and communicative conventions, and conveys their own messages and meanings. . . . The underlying meaning of female graffiti is that they express the co-operation of the dominated and reflect the strategy of mutual help employed by those in a subordinate status. (1980, pp. 249-259)

Many persons also use the walls for affirmation and counsel. Such graffitists reflect a compelling need to be transparent to the world (Fraser, 1980), which suggests that many graffitists use the medium to perform a vital human function. Research reveals that suppressing disclosure of extremely personal and traumatic experiences to others over a long period is unnatural and disease-causing (e.g., Blotchy, Carscanddon, & Grandmaison, 1983; Garcia & Geisler, 1988; Jourard, 1971; Stiles, Shuster, & Harrigan, 1992). Greenberg and Stone (1992) found that persons who wrote about severe traumas reported fewer physical symptoms than low-severity trauma subjects and tended to report fewer symptoms than control subjects. Pennebaker and Beall (1986) also found that subjects instructed to write about past traumatic events report fewer health center visits following the experiment compared with controls who wrote about trivial events.

Other research is equally revealing. Gilmar and Brown (1983) found that a class of high school students used graffiti to reveal their deepest concerns: "Silently the words clamor for our attention. They are a key to the locked door, which when opened shows us their humor, cynicism, faith, and despair" (p. 45). The students found that graffiti opened discourse among classmates with whom they shared no other meaningful relationship. In addition, Shulman, Peven, and Byrne (1973) found graffiti to be an effective means of promoting communication between patients and staff in a mental health unit in Chicago. The graffiti provided the staff with clues about how to approach and treat each patient. Shulman and colleagues concluded that the anonymity allows patients to express what otherwise might be inhibited by fear, convention, and embarrassment.

The endless motives behind graffiti production show the complex nature of human action. Collectively, all the different motives show human beings acting deliberately and purposely upon the world. The walls are used creatively to satisfy existential needs for transparency and community. In addition, graffiti, particularly the graffiti of disenfranchised and marginalized groups, show human beings stubbornly resisting hierarchy, domination, and coercion.

Gaylin and Jennings also fail to offer any critical analysis of the social and material context that surrounds the social problems that coercion and control are supposedly necessary to correct. In this way, these authors foster the impression that social problems occur in a vacuum. But what of the emergent forms of social control and coercion that are contributing to the pauperization of peoples? What kind of social control and coercion will this kind of pauperization soon demand? What kind of morality legitimizes the social control and coercion that allows so few to possess so much and so many to have less and less? What of the morality that permits the pauperization reflected by urban decay, blight, and hopelessness? Further, what of the effects of a status quo that deliberately blankets our humanity with notions of competition over cooperation? Indeed, what are the effects of a society that elevates wants over needs? In the end, how does all of this affect the ethics and morality of social control and coercion between different groups?

By shifting the focus away from the factors contributing to wealth disparity between the top and the bottom, and by that the blight that overwhelms those at the bottom, Gaylin and Jennings also shift culpability from the top to the bottom of society. Open season is declared on those at the bottom with regard to condemnation and persecution. The top, on the other hand, goes unscathed, along with the material and discursive practices that confer all kinds of privileges. What emerges are justifications for harsher measures to correct the behaviors of those at the bottom. In sum, Gaylin and Jennings neglect a tremendous body of research that points to a significant relationship between many social problems and the distribution of wealth and resources.

Gaylin and Jennings fault the ethos of autonomy for the degradation of the human condition. But as autonomy is a myth, this criticism is off the mark. What Gaylin and Jennings are describing as the pitfalls of the autonomy ethos are actually the effects of extant social relations and practices. In other words, the problem is alienation. In *The Anatomy of Human Destructiveness*, Erich Fromm offers a compelling description of alienation:

> By alienation is meant a mode of experience in which the person experiences himself [sic] as an alien. He has become, one might say, estranged from himself. He does not experience himself as the center of his world, as the creator of his own acts—but his acts and their consequences have become his masters, whom he obeys, or whom he may even worship. The alienated person is out of touch with himself as he is out of touch with any other person. He, like the others, are experienced as things are experienced; with the senses and with common sense, but at the same time without being related to oneself and to the world outside productively. (pp. 120-121)

Alienation is the surrender of our power to our creations. It undercuts our ability and willingness to confront the power of the few. The effect is coercion and social control. Fromm writes:

> Alienation as we find it in modern society is almost total; it pervades the relationship of man to his work, to the things he consumes, to the state, to his fellow man, and to himself. Man has created a world of man-made things as it never existed before. He has constructed a complicated social machine to administer the technical machine he built. Yet this whole creation of his stands over and above him. He does not feel himself as a creator and center, but as the servant of a Golem, which his hands have built. The more powerful and gigantic the forces are which he unleashes, the more powerless he feels himself as a human being. He confronts himself with his own forces embodied in things he has created, alienated from himself. He is owned by his own creation, and has lost ownership of himself. (1973, pp. 124-125)

Alienation reduces us to objects. It dehumanizes us. It erases the complexity of our humanity. It stops us from questioning and acting on our questions. Its most potent effect, however, is the undermining of our faith in a better tomorrow. With that our ability and willingness to fight are diminished. The result is fatalism and nihilism. It is for these reasons that alienation poses such a pernicious threat to our well-being. But, in fact, power never leaves our person. Disempowerment is actually a set of complex schemes, both material and discursive, that makes for the illusion that power is beyond us. According to Clegg, "The greatest achievement of power is its reification. When power is regarded as thing-like, as something solid, real and material, as something an agent has, then this represents power in its most pervasive and concrete mode" (1989, p. 207).

Gaylin and Jennings contend that our affective constitution hinders the effectiveness of behavioral modification programs devoid of social control and coercion. This supposedly accounts for why such programs perform dismally. In other words, the fault rests with the overwhelming appeal to reason. But this analysis completely misses the mark. Undoubtedly, a better explanation is that such programs address the symptoms rather than the causes of the problems.

But what of the success of those programs that target those at the top of the hierarchy? It is troubling enough that Gaylin and Jennings focus disproportionately on a particular group, but that this group comprises the weakest among us—as regards to opportunity and allocation of resources—is most troubling. In fact, this exclusive focus on those at the bottom is blatantly unfair. Gaylin and Jennings never offer any explanation for their monomaniacal focus on those at the bottom. Fairness demands that Gaylin and Jennings consider all groups. It would be interesting to know the effects of social control and coercion on greed and discriminatory behavior.

What is also troubling is how Gaylin and Jennings account for the hierarchal ordering of society. We are given exactly what Richard Herrnstein and Charles Murray give us: IQ. Interestingly, however, Gaylin and Jennings never explicate the consequences of such a position in the way Herrnstein and Murray do. There is an apparent unwillingness to be forthright about the relationship among genetics, social control and coercion, deviancy, social policy, and hierarchy.

Gaylin and Jennings contend that low IQ is responsible for criminality and deviancy. This contention legitimizes the exercise of coercion upon a select group and, as a result, perpetuates a deep distrust of our humanity. The obvious extension is eugenics, but out of fear of social punishment many persons are afraid to broach the subject openly. However, as long as the relationship between IQ and criminality is seen as a truth, and criminal activity continues to rise, the full legitimacy of this discussion—the proximity of which is evidenced by the success of *The Bell Curve*—will no doubt eventually occur. The linking of IQ with criminality is encouraged by the existing intellectual context that is predisposed to this kind of claim. IQ offers an easy explanation of criminality. The linking of IQ with criminality poses no threat to the status quo. It sustains our deep distrust and suspicion of our humanity. Accordingly, the discursive and material practices that engender urban blight, hopelessness, and poverty go uninterrogated.

It is tempting to now turn our attention to debunking the legitimacy of IQ. But, again, the fact that this beast keeps appearing and reappearing—after many believed that the matter had been finally put to rest—shows that something about this argument is deeply appealing to us. Indeed, the fact that this claim can reappear again and again and gain such widespread appeal and respectability on even the most fraudulent kind of research shows how amenable our society is to such kinds of claims. In *The Bell Curve Wars*, a compilation of essays on the controversy emanating from Herrnstein and Murray's *The Bell Curve*, Randall Kennedy of Harvard Law School makes such a point:

> Much of *The Bell Curve*'s power derives from Murray-Herrnstein's success in tapping into a widespread yearning for explanation and guidance that accepts the claim of cognitive racial inferiority as at least plausible. *The Bell Curve* would not have attracted the attention it has unless the diagnosis it offered was considered to be within the pale of respectable discussion by important arbiters of opinion. . . . It is the perceived plausibility of *The Bell Curve*'s racial analysis that prompts arbiters of public opinion to give *The Bell Curve* a hearing. Despite considerable disagreement with it, the notion of black intellectual inferiority is still sufficiently alive to be deemed suitable for serious debate. (1995, p. 184)

The warm reception must also be seen against the fact that this nation boasts a special affinity with God, with endless efforts to end whatever separation exists between government and religion. Indeed, the religious quarter and other usually vocal proponents of family values never took Herrnstein and Murray to task, even for the kinds of cruel policy recommendations that the book contains. The point is that regurgitating all of the volumes of research that debunk IQ is futile. Nothing positive will be gained from doing so. As long as a deep distrust of our humanity exists, nearly any kind of explanation suffices to justify our belief that hierarchy is good.

Communibiology

Natural selection theory now infects communication theory. In a featured address to the National Communication Association, James McCroskey, Professor of Communication, West Virginia University, said: "[N]o theory of human interaction can be taken seriously unless it is informed by this massive body of research literature that already established strong effects for inborn, individual differences in neurobiological processes that underlie major dimensions of social behavior" (1998, p. 8). The research that McCroskey is referring to is that of psychobiology and neurobiology. A bedrock proposition of communibiology is that "The neurobiological structures underlying temperament traits and individual differences are mostly inherited" (1998, p. 48). Beatty and McCroskey posit that verbal aggressiveness reflects our aggressive and violent nature:

> In concrete terms, individuals high in verbal aggressiveness are highly motivated to achieve goals through interpersonal interaction, quickly turn to aggressive tactics when initial attempts fail, and without sufficient inhibition, become highly aggressive. The attentional focus, which accompanies system activation, promotes persistent focus on the goal and minimizes focus on potential negative consequences of aggressive symbolic action. (1997, p. 453)

About the need for this turn to nature in the communication field, McCroskey says the following:

> It is clear that science is producing one breakthrough after another which indicates the powerful impact of genetics on human traits. Many of these traits are the foundation of human interaction. We cannot continue to ignore what is going on around us. Conducting our learning experiments and writing our insightful ethnographies will not make us relevant in a future we can now see—a society that understands and adapts to the fact that much of human communication behavior is genetically influenced and

difficult to control or change. . . . however, if the failure to learn certain communication skills is not the cause of a problem, our normal skills-training course is not likely to be the solution. This is why I call for a shift of emphasis to the communibiological perspective in both our scholarship and teaching. (1998, pp. 8-9)

Beatty and McCroskey (1997) contend that only communibiology is consistent with what is supposedly now known about neurological functioning, which is to say that goals, motives, and intentions are supposedly artifacts of cognitive processes. According to Beatty and McCroskey:

If we insist that communicators are goal-oriented, we must tackle the question of first cause: Where do intention, motives, and goals originate if not within the neurobiological structures of the brain? If we insist that we can exert control over our cognitive process or make choices, where does the control and the decision to exert it or make choices originate if not in brain structures? The alternative position is to posit the existence of some entity in control of brain processes, capable of independent cognition. . . . (1997, p. 448)

In other words, no mind exists. It is all about forces acting upon our set neurological structures. Cognition is merely an effect of such an arrangement. Volition, too, is delegitimized. All of our motives and behaviors begin and end with our biology ("Unless a person's biology changes, we expect reasonably consistent forms of responses"). According to Beatty and McCroskey:

[T]he communibiological perspective acknowledges that communicators are first and foremost biological entities. We do not somehow transcend our brain structures when we interact. Neurobiological composition limits and restricts our range of responses just as our genetic profile limits our maximum height or ability to understand complex mathematics. From this vantage point, research findings are interpreted from a biological frame of reference. Thus, when research findings conflict with our biological principles, we favor the biological explanation. Accordingly, attentiveness to biology is not merely an alternative or supplemental analysis, it is fundamental to the concept of traits. . . . (1998, p. 59)

In this way, and as Beatty and McCroskey admit, communibiology is decidedly reductionistic. In fact, as with other strident proponents of natural selection theory, reductionism is celebrated. Again, reductionism erases any existential relations between us and our discursive and nondiscursive worlds. We can supposedly be decoupled from the complex web of relations that embed us. To do so merely demands obtaining the correct means to extract the various causal forces that set our behavior.

The primary means of extraction is operationalization. This is the process of making concepts measurable. It is assumed that all relevant concepts—because they are unalterable by environmental forces—can be reliably measured. Consequently, when problems arise with testing and measuring, such as obtaining a consistent measure, the fault rests with the instrument rather than with the concept (Lewontin, Rose, & Kamin, 1984). The problem, however, is that adherents to this perspective miss the circularity that undergirds operationalization. In brief, what instruments capture is what concepts the instruments were meant to capture. So, the fact that Beatty and McCroskey's instrument supposedly captures verbal aggressiveness is purely a result—of course, after much testing and retesting—that the instrument is shaped to capture that concept. As a result, verbal aggressiveness becomes what verbal aggressiveness tests measure.

Communibiology takes circular reasoning to new extremes. McCroskey writes, "Research in this area [neurobiology and psychobiology] suggests that our traits drive our qualitative scholarship, just as they drive our other communication behavior" (1998, p. 11). On the other hand, however, McCroskey also contends that behavior is decidedly unalterable by environment, and that our extant view of the social world hinders the progress of communication theory and inquiry. It seems that our nature damns the progress of communication theory. If, moreover, our responses are set by our biology, to what or whom is McCroskey and company appealing for getting us to accept communibiology over other perspectives? On the other hand, how did McCroskey and company escape the hold of our nature? If, moreover, our nature has such a firm grip on us, as adherents of communibiology claim, what becomes our means of determining validity other than what our nature dictates? In other words, what becomes of objectivity, a notion cherished by proponents of reductionism and operationalization? How would the truths of communibiology be objectively analyzed? In the end, McCroskey and company contend that a turn to nature is good for us because our nature supposedly says so. In my view, this represents the most circular of arguments. It is probably because of this new-found level of circularity that McCroskey and company never address the enormous body of literature that criticizes the turn to nature for explanations of human behavior.

Instruments of the kind that McCroskey and company use have other structural problems. Such instruments supposedly allow for comparisons among respondents. Results are used, for example, to claim that certain persons are either more or less verbally aggressive than others. Such comparisons allow Beatty and McCroskey to posit, for example, the following:

> Verbal aggressiveness as temperamental expression implies that compared to individuals low in trait verbal aggressiveness, high scorers on verbal aggression instruments engage in aggressive communication more because the neurobiological circuitry underlying their behavioral systems requires comparatively less stimulation to facilitate and more stimulation to inhibit aggressive responses. (1997, p. 453)

In reality, however, such comparisons are illusional. As Lewontin, Rose, and Kamin astutely observe, "The fact that it is possible to devise tests on which individuals score arbitrary points does not mean that the quality being measured by the test is really metric" (1984, p. 92). Scales that afford comparisons are ordinal. Moreover, such scales are also arbitrary, which is to say that the measures on the scales are social constructions. What scores make for different representations of aggressiveness are created by people. Put another way, what differences exist between levels of verbal aggressiveness are purely arbitrary. The researcher simply assumes that different levels of verbal aggressiveness exist. The illusion makes us believe that the instruments are capturing different levels of verbal aggressiveness that exist independent of the researcher.

The reality is that environment plays a significant part in shaping our reality—our beliefs, values, assumptions, fears, hopes, and so forth that fashion what our instruments capture and reflect. Discursivity shapes the measurement, meaning, and politicization of all concepts, no matter how real. We bring values, beliefs, fears, and so forth to the identifying, shaping, and understanding of concepts. It is most possible that a particular people can look at verbal aggressiveness differently, and possibly even so differently as to make any kind of reasonable comparison impossible. In fact, a particular people can have a worldview that simply encumbers the evolution of a particular concept. This is a reality that anthropologists have long known.

Communibiology also has problems with communication. To look at communication as an artifact of being leads naturally to a fixation on how messages are produced, packaged, and transmitted. Communication becomes expression rather than the constituting element of being human. In other words, communication as an artifact of being assumes no kind of sacred relation between communication and being. It is unreflectively assumed that being can be divorced from communication. In reality, however, such separation is impossible. Being and communication are intertwined. Human beings are constituted through communication. Being is manifest through communication. The point is that communibiology provides a meaningless view of communication. It tells us absolutely nothing about communication. It completely misunderstands its ostensible subject matter. It is really no perspective about communication, but merely represents another expression of psychobiological and neurobiological "truths." Communication is seen as simply an effect of our neurobiological structures. It is an artifact of being. It presumably has no real and significant bearing on the genesis of our humanity. Communibiology provides no ethical foundation to justify compassion, empathy, love, equality, cooperation, and diversity. It depoliticizes communication. It undercuts the study of communication by reducing communication to merely an effect of neurobiology.

McCroskey and company display equally damning misunderstanding of biology. It is simply wrong to posit that genes deterministically fashion human behavior. This error shows a blatant ignorance of a text-book distinction between *genotype* and *phenotype*. Biologists have scolded psychobiologists harshly for this kind of ignorance. As Lewontin, Rose, and Kamin explain:

> The critical distinction in biology is between the phenotype of an organism, which may be taken to mean the total of its morphological, physiological, and behavioral properties, and its genotype, the state of its genes. It is the genotype, not the phenotype, that is inherited. The genotype is fixed; the phenotype develops and changes constantly. The organism itself is at every stage the consequence of a developmental process that occurs in some historical sequence of environments. At every instant in development (and development goes on until death) the next step is a consequence of the organism's present biological state, which includes both its genes and the physical and social environment in which it finds itself. This comprises the first principle of developmental genetics: that every organism is the unique product of the interaction between genes and environment at every stage of life. (1984, p. 95)

The evolution of communibiology shows why biologists are increasingly expressing concern about the misrepresentation of biology by sociobiologists and others. Ruth Hubbard, Professor of Biology at Harvard University, writes: "At present, I spend much of my time countering claims that exaggerate the significance of genes and DNA. Looking upon genes as control centers for various characteristics or activities within the body obscures the extent to which the functioning of genes depends on other substances and on physical and social forces. It also misrepresents the complex way that genes relate to health, disease, and behavior" (1998, p. B6). Communibiology represents the increasing *geneticization* of our society. Looking to genes to deal with our many social problems represents too attractive a notion to dismiss casually. It makes for easy explanations and solutions to such problems. It depoliticizes being. It makes no real demands on the status quo.

SUMMARY AND CONCLUSION

Sociobiologists, sociosexologists, psychobiologists, communibiologists, and others who posit a deep distrust and suspicion of our humanity make no compelling argument to justify hierarchy. The popular success of such perspectives is no doubt rooted in their resonance with our deepest fears. Our deep distrust and suspicion of our humanity is legitimized. Our dysfunctional behavior receives moral and theoretical cover. Selfishness, greed, deceit, deception, and so forth are now virtues rather than evils. Hierarchy is good. Competition is good. Market forces are great. In this way, this emergent secular movement legitimizes the status quo. It demands nothing from us. It also provides apparently easy answers to the many social problems that human beings confront. Witness the increasing concentration of research funds—by diverting funds from research on the contribution of environment to human behavior—to find the genetic basis of violent and deviant human behavior. The cover of a recent issue of *U.S. News & World Report* about "How the politics of biology shapes opinion, policy, and our self image," had a baby dressed in striped prison garb—prison number, cap, and all. In a featured article, Wray Herbert pointed out that major institutions are now "proposing . . . a biomedical approach to criminal justice [that] shows how far the intellectual pendulum has swung towards biology" (1997, p. 74). Also, a new book, *Demonic Males: Apes and the*

Origins of Human Violence, by Richard Wrangham and Dale Peterson (1996), relates the violent behavior of chimpanzees to that of humans. What will surely lend credibility to this thesis and to the success of the book (which has already been widely and positively reviewed), is the fact that Wrangham is a professor of biological anthropology at Harvard University.

Another new book, *Bonobo: The Forgotten Ape,* by Frans B. M. de Waal, professor of psychology at Emory University, also relates our behavior to that of apes. In a previous book, *Chimpanzee Politics: Power and Sex Among Apes,* which was also well received, de Waal elaborated on our supposedly selfish and competitive nature, a view he derived, of course, from studying chimpanzees. His new book is about bonobos. According to de Waal, "Traditional scenarios have depicted humans as hunters and warriors who conquered the world through genocide. Other primate societies, such as those of baboons and chimpanzees, may lend support to these views, but the lives of bonobos most certainly do not. If chimpanzees are from Mars, then bonobos must be from Venus" (1997, p. B7). His findings reveal that bonobos tend to be egalitarian and pacifist, show high regard for the concerns of others, and females occupy the dominant positions of power. All of this leads de Waal to add, "If a species so close to us, can dramatically deviate from the male-bonded, male-dominated pattern that scenarios of human evolution often take for granted, we must have more flexibility in our lineage than scholars used to assume." In the end, Alan Wolfe may be correct after all, "The idea that human behavior, however complex, is at root a form of animal behavior is too powerful an idea ever to disappear" (1993, p. 51).

The fact that hierarchy enjoys legitimacy across theoretical, political, and spiritual perspectives points to a sharing of a common worldview. We must ask, what is the validity of this worldview that sustains hierarchy? What are the origins of the political/social/theoretical/ ideological context that sustains this deep distrust and suspicion of our humanity? Our attention now turns to this matter.

3

Liberation,
Worldviews & Ideology

Human beings are paradigm beings. Paradigms are ways of viewing. Woven within each view are various assumptions, values, and beliefs about the world. Paradigms supply conceptual ground for our discursive and material practices. They fashion our understandings and our relations to the world, and set forth our relations to each other. Paradigms encompass what is commonly known as *ideology*, our unconscious assumptions about the world that shape our perceptions of situations and events (Deetz & Kersten, 1983). Ideology shapes what enters our reality, what is good and what is bad, and what is possible (Therborn, 1980). We focus now on the origins of the paradigm that gives legitimacy to hierarchy and coercion. What are the origins of our deep distrust and suspicion of our humanity? What is the ideology that this paradigm engenders?

I make a distinction between the *emergent* paradigm and the *dominant* paradigm. Our extant paradigm is the latter. Others use the terms "Old Story" and "New Story." I focus only on how the different paradigms deal with the question of coercion. The emergent paradigm represents the evolution of a worldview devoid of the distrust and suspicion that our extant paradigm posits. In this way, the emergent paradigm presents a theoretical opportunity to consider the end of hierarchy.

THE DOMINANT PARADIGM

The dominant paradigm represents our extant ways of viewing and being in the world. It is the well from which all of our extant discursive and material practices spring. It is the paradigm that shapes our understanding of the world and sets forth our relation to each other. The dominant paradigm has a strident dualist ethos. Arguably the most dominant dualism is that between us and the world. Other dualisms are energy and matter, order and chaos, and male and female.

All dualisms are hierarchal. In this way, order is superior to chaos, energy superior to matter, and so forth. For example, Pythagoras believed that "There is a good principle that has created order, light and man, and a bad principle which has created chaos, darkness and women." Francis Bacon, a primary articulator of the dominant paradigm, said, "Matter is not devoid of an appetite and inclination to dissolve the world and fall back into the old Chaos. [It therefore must be] restrained and kept in order by the prevailing concord of things." Consequently, each dualism posits an uneven distribution of power or an active and passive component; energy controls matter, cause controls effects, mind controls body, order controls chaos, and so on. In short, one component is always superior to the other. Without energy, matter is supposedly random. That the world reflects order is testament that energy imposes order, and thereby constitutes the means to control and fashion matter nonrandomly and predictably. The notion that energy both controls and brings order to matter becomes the foundation of *linearity* and *causality*, both bedrock assumptions of the dominant paradigm. The notion of causality posits that A determines what happens to B, or, B is shaped by A. It posits a relationship of domination (A) and subordination (B), that is, a hierarchical relation between A and B. The fact that A supposedly controls the destiny and faith of B means that A is dominant.

The reasoning and assumptions that undergird the dominant paradigm engender the belief that the human condition and the non-human world (another dualism) is subject to manipulation and control, pending the ability to attain desired *effects* by identifying the matching *causes*. As Nobel Laureate Ilya Prigogine and Isabelle Stengers explain, "This science [dominant paradigm] provides the means for systematically acting on the world, for predicting and modifying the course of natural processes, for conceiving devices that can harness and exploit the forces and material resources of nature" (1984, p. 37). According to Andre Gorz:

Western science, as it presently exists, is inadequate to all these [liberatory] tasks. It does not offer us the intellectual and material tools to exercise self-determination, self-administration, self-rule, in any field. It is an expert science, monopolized by the professionals and estranged from the people. And this situation after all is not surprising—Western science was never intended for the people. Its main relevance, from the beginning, was . . . to dominate workers, not to make them free. (1980, p. 272)

Hierarchy distills our view of the world and even our own humanity with notions of domination, subordination, and manipulation. Inevitably, a world that is understood hierarchically becomes a world that is also organized hierarchically. In *Toward an Ecological Society*, Murray Bookchin succinctly makes this point:

The self in hierarchical society not only lives, acts, and communicates hierarchically; it thinks and feels hierarchically by organizing the vast diversity of sense data, memory, values, passions, and thought along hierarchical lines. Differences between things, people, and relations do not exist as ends in themselves; they are organized hierarchically in the mind itself and pitted against each other antagonistically in varying degrees of dominance and obedience even when they could be complementary to each other in the prevailing reality. (1980, pp. 268-269)

The result is that hierarchy splits the human condition by reifying a mind/body duality. That which is supposedly of the mind (e.g., reason) is elevated and that which is supposedly of the body (e.g., passion) is subjugated. Reason emerges as the preeminent path to *truth*, whereas the body becomes subject to subordination and coercion. It is commonly believed that without any disciplining of the body, promiscuity and chaos will reign. Simply put, reason is pitted against sensuality. In this way, the dominant paradigm hierarchically fragments the world and our humanity. About this fragmentation, David Bohm, one of the foremost theoretical physicists of this century, writes:

The notion that all these fragments are separately existent is evidently an illusion, and this illusion cannot do other than lead to endless conflict and confusion. Indeed, the attempt to live according to the notion that the fragments are really separate is, in essence, what has led to the growing series of extremely urgent crises that is confronting us today. Thus, as is now well known, this way of life has brought about pollution, world-wide economic and political disorder, and the creation of an overall environment that is neither physically nor mentally healthy for most of the people who have to live in it. Individually, there has developed a widespread feeling of helplessness and despair in the face of what seems to be an overwhelming mass of disparate social forces, going beyond the control and even the comprehension of the human beings who are caught up in it. (1980, pp. 1-2)

The hopelessness and despair that Bohm describes result from the alienation that a dualist ethos engenders. Though Bohm never uses the term alienation, he provides an apt account:

[W]hen this mode of thought is applied more broadly to man's notion of himself and the whole world in which he lives (i.e., to his self-world), then man ceases to regard the resulting divisions as merely useful or convenient and begins to see and experience himself and his world as actually constituted of separately existent fragments. Being guided by a fragmentary self-world view, man then acts in such a way as to try to break himself and the world up, so that all seems to correspond to his way of thinking. Man thus obtains an apparent proof of the correctness of his fragmentary self-world view though, of course, he overlooks the fact that it is he himself, acting according to his mode of thought, who has brought about the fragmentation that now seems to have an autonomous existence, independent of his will and of his desire. (1980, pp. 2-3)

Probably the most egregious act perpetrated by the dominant paradigm is the moral sanctioning of domination and exploitation. This sanctioning obstructs any questioning of the ethics, morality, and human consequences of domination and exploitation. In fact, the logos of the dominant paradigm is so tightly woven as to prohibit any such questioning. The result is endless discourses about ethics, morality, and equality that never question the legitimacy of coercion. The only demand is that the domination and exploitation be kinder and gentler, or that coercion be used properly (e.g., Gaylin & Jennings).

Common understandings of organizing reflect the dominant paradigm. Organizing is seen as a means to an end. It is about achieving goals through the collective effort of many human beings. The focus is on tasks. In this way, organizing is commonly understood as planning, organization, command, coordination, and control. The primary objective is always for a few to control many. Such an arrangement reflects the long held belief that the many will act in ways that threaten the interest of the few when left to their own volition. George Bonello writes, "What has become increasingly evident . . . is that it is not efficiency which dictates the organizational forms of industry so much as *efficiency of control*" (1992, p. 39; emphasis in original). The dominant paradigm makes believe that a select group (the few) with the proper skills and techniques can control the actions and behaviors of the common mortals (the many). As a case in point, George Barnett, Professor of Communication, State University of New York at Buffalo, posits that Galileo, a mathematically dimensional analysis system, can change an organization's culture (i.e., organizational members' ways of being):

> This procedure will help an organization change the direction of, and the variance within, its culture. Directionally, focus may be changed away from the dysfunctional aspects [!] of the culture and toward the goal as defined by management in the statements of corporate philosophy. . . . This technique provides a message strategy which, when applied consistently, would reduce culture variation. (1988, pp. 116-117)

This claim aptly captures the ethos of the dominant paradigm. Barnett obviously sees nothing fundamentally wrong with coercion, domination, manipulation, and subordination. He apparently sees mechanisms such as Galileo as essential for the making of the good organization and the good society. His apparent lack of any moral reservation surrounding the uses of such kinds of manipulation plainly shows how the dominant paradigm forecloses any questioning whatsoever of the morality and ethics of domination, manipulation, and subordination.

Barnett's proposed application of the Galileo system represents the belief that capital has the moral authority and legitimacy to fashion our behavior. However, what about those behaviors that labor deems functional and capital deems dysfunctional, such as slaves' destruction of plantation property, or sabotaging efforts by concentration camp laborers, or any other kind of behavior that labor finds suitable to deal with undesirable behavior on the part of capital? Based on what Galileo represents, all resistant acts are dysfunctional. But what morality stops capital from employing Galileo against labor cruelly and excessively? What is the origin and calculus of this morality upon which labor must depend? Barnett's views imply that the morality of capital is somehow superior to that of labor, just as Gaylin and Jennings assume that superior morality inheres in the academic, economic, and political realms. However, countless examples show the fallibility of the kind of determinism that undergirds the dominant paradigm. Native Americans' history of jumping off mountains to avoid exploitation by settlers, and the myriad of tactics that slaves employed to destroy the plantation system, including abortions and suicides, represent just a few compelling examples of the capacity of human beings to resist manipulation and exploitation.

The consistent resistance by the many against the few lends further support to the thesis that coercion will always meet such tactics. Oppression threatens self-preservation. In other words, a power that seeks manipulation and control will always confront another power (determinism/instinct) that seeks growth and liberation. Stewart Clegg observes:

> Power and resistance stand in relationship to each other. . . . One rarely has one without the other. . . . There is always a dialectic to power, always another agency, another set of standing conditions pertinent to the realization of that agency's causal powers against the resistance of another. . . . Where there is organization, there will be resistance, as well as power, contradiction induced by control, rationalities instead of rationality and passions as well as interests. (1989, pp. 166-167)

Galileo is a political artifact. It is an artifact of a paradigm that legitimizes coercion, domination, and manipulation. It is, however, the notion of objectivity that masks the moral and political nature of Galileo. Objectivity legitimizes the status quo. It cloaks the human costs of domination, manipulation, and subordination by bolstering the hegemony of the dominant paradigm and upholding scientism as the only path to truth. ("The phenomenon is always right.") It blocks moral scrutiny of the alienation and disempowerment that the status quo engenders. This explains why Barnett is oblivious to the ethical and moral concerns presented by Galileo. His primary concern is the effectiveness (effects) of the technology (causes). But this is exactly what the dominant paradigm engenders, a belief that objective truth is superior to and apart from morality. Supposedly, morality is subjective, whereas truth is objective. However, our discursive nature mediates our world—even our best observations of the world are relational. As Wolfgang Smith observes, "There can be no bona fide observation without the theoretical aspect of the enterprise coming into play. One might put it this way: To observe in the sense of the physicist is to pass from the perceptible to the imperceptible—and only theory can span the gap" (1995, p. 33). In other words, human beings are devoid of the means to mirror the world. However, our subjectivity should be seen against a world that is extremely complex, with limitless potential for the evolution of new forms and meanings. It is an extraordinary world with a potency, richness, depth, and fecundity that surpasses anything that our own human capability can ever muster. Our subjectivity offers endless meanings of the world.

This emergent view fosters dialogical understandings of the world. In other words, our truths are dialogical because our relation to the world is dialogical. As such, our truths exist within the context of dialogical action. Put another way, the fact that truth is dialogical means that truth is also a question of morality—that is, a statement about values. According to Paulo Freire, a dialogical conception of truth affords a dialogical theory of pedagogy—that is, a pedagogy that engenders liberation, rather than domination and manipulation:

> Education as the practice of freedom—as opposed to education as the practice of domination—denies that man [sic] is abstract, isolated, independent, and unattached to the world; it also denies that the world exists as a reality apart from people. Authentic reflection considers neither abstract man nor the world without people, but people in their relations with the world. In these relations consciousness and world are simultaneous: consciousness neither precedes the world nor follows it. (1993, p. 62)

To get beyond hierarchy, a paradigm shift is necessary. This is obviously the only way of dismantling the cosmology of coercion. An emergent paradigm presents the opportunity to consider different ways of being. I use the term "emergent paradigm" to refer to a compendium of different arguments, many with even conflicting positions and points of contention, that break one way or the other with the bedrock assumptions that undergird the dominant paradigm. I, again, limit the following discussion to that which is pertinent to the notions of coercion and hierarchy.

THE EMERGENT PARADIGM

The emergent paradigm does away with the bifurcating ethos that pervades the dominant paradigm. Instead, the world is seen as a reservoir of *unitive consciousness*. So, "What, then, is a physical object?" According to Wolfgang Smith, "Nothing more, nor less, one is now bound to admit, than a particular manifestation of the total reality. *Qua* physical object, to be sure, it exists in space and time, and exhibits a certain phenomenal identity; and yet, in itself, it transcends these bounds, and that apparent identity" (1995, p. 71). The emergent paradigm also posits that our ability to bring meaning to bear on the world releases us from any fixed meaning of the cosmos. In this way, human beings are seen as having the ability to contribute to the completion of the cosmos.

Amit Goswami, Professor of Physics at the Institute of Theoretical Sciences at the University of Oregon, believes that our emergent understanding suggests that the cosmos was created for human beings. It is, after all, only human beings who can construct meaning. In *The Self-Aware Universe*, he writes:

> It is time to recognize the archetypal nature of mankind's creation myths (found in the Book of Genesis in the Judeo-Christian tradition, in the Vedas of the Hindu tradition, and in many other religious traditions). The cosmos was created for our sake. Such myths are compatible with quantum physics, not contradictory. (1993, p. 141)

The emergent paradigm stresses an ethos of holism. This is obviously different from the ethos of apartness—through duality—that the dominant paradigm encourages. According to Goswami:

> The shortcomings of dualism are well known. Notably, it cannot explain how a separate, nonmaterial mind interacts with a material body. If there are such mind-body interactions, then there have to be exchanges of energy between the two domains. In myriad experiments, we find that the energy of the material universe by itself remains a constant (this is the law of conservation of energy). Neither has any evidence shown that energy is lost to or gained from the mental domain. How can that be if there are interactions going on between the two domains? (p. 51)

Wolfgang Smith writes, "[W]hat we have termed the physical universe, the nature of which we speak is not to be conceived as a domain or ensemble made up of physical objects. To be sure, physical objects do exist; the point, however, is that these objects partake somewhat of relativity, and are to be viewed, not as so many independent entities, but as diverse manifestations of a single and unbroken reality" (1995, p. 67). David Bohm puts the matter this way:

> [T]he classical idea of the separability of the world into distinct but interacting parts is no longer valid or relevant. Rather, we have to regard the universe as *an undivided and unbroken whole.* Division into particles, or into particles and fields, is only a crude abstraction and approximation. Thus, we come to an order that is radically different from that of Galileo and Newton—the order of *undivided wholeness.* (1980, pp. 124-125)

Any kind of division engenders alienation. Alienation, again, represents the transfer of our life forces to our creation. It undercuts our ability to act upon the world. It also undercuts our ability to bring forth new meanings. Our fecundity, spontaneity, and creativity are all undermined. We become less human and act accordingly. An ethos of division makes for supposed differences that foster racial conflict, gender conflict, sexual orientation conflict, tribal conflict, and so forth. In other words, gender, sexual orientation, and ethnicity are all artifacts of fragmentation. When duality disappears, the notion of apartness also disappears, and with this the undermining of our supposed ability to understand the world objectively. What then becomes of our methodology and our ability to *discover* the truth? The emergent paradigm posits *a faculty of unmediated vision* that allows for an understanding of the universal through the particular. Smith explains:

> The great fact is that the physical universe is not after all an unmitigated contingency. . . . And this implies that physics is in reality concerned, not with particular existents as such, but with particulars insofar as these exhibit a universal principle or law. Whatever may be left over remains of necessity unknown. Thus, what physics seeks, and is able to grasp in its own fashion, is the necessary in the contingent, or the eternal in the ephemeral, as one can also say. (1995, pp. 34-36)

Nobody knows exactly what the paradigm shift will demand of us. Understandably, this makes for a natural fear of the unknown, and with that a certain amount of anxiety. But probably the most difficult thing to accept is the humility that comes with accepting the fact that humans cannot gain dominion over the world. This is against everything that the dominant paradigm represents. To entertain seriously the notion of a unitive consciousness is to enter the realm of the spiritual.

The emergent paradigm posits that this is a world of potentiality. This potentiality represents a self organizing and self evolving calculus that is dialectically and organically guiding the evolution of the natural world. Indeed, findings from the social, natural, and physical sciences reveal that all naturally evolving systems possess a ceaseless self-organizing and self-evolving capability. Stability and equilibrium are nonexistent. What stability exists is found only within evolutionary paths and schemes. As such, only evolution and disequilibrium are constant.

The evolutionary process reflects both linearity and nonlinearity. In other words, although the process is constant, creativity guides the process. Persons from all theoretical and philosophical persuasions are baffled by the tremendous level of creativity, and yes, wonder, that each new discovery of the evolutionary self-organizing process brings forth. The origin of this fecundity is the big point of contention. It seems that the fecundity of the world is simply limitless.

The evolutionary self-organizing process is neither random nor haphazard. The process ceaselessly aspires toward greater and greater levels of complexity. Accordingly, trying to extract linear and stable relationships between or among variables is useless, as all such relationships disappear. Even trying to do so strips away all the other relationships and dynamics that are concomitantly evolving, constructing, and maintaining the complexity that is constituting reality. Evelyn Fox Keller, author of *Reflections on Gender and Science*, believes that "the conception of nature as orderly, and not merely law bound, allows nature itself to be generative and resourceful—more complex and abundant than we can either describe or prescribe. In this alternative view, nature comes to be seen as an active partner in a more reciprocal relation to an observer, equally active, but neither omniscient nor omnipotent" (1985, p. 134).

The emergent paradigm rejects the notion that the truths of this world are transferable to numbers and formal theory. The world and human beings are seen as too complex, too fluid, too uncertain, too nonlinear, for reductionism. Instead, the emergent paradigm views all truth construction artifacts and processes as poetics and politics. According to Wallerstein, "The object is to construct an interpretation of complex reality by surpassing the simple generalizations, interweaving them, and defining the degree of their relevance" (1992, p. 6). To account for the aspiration toward complexity, the contention is that complexity catalyzes and safeguards the evolution of the potential. Higher levels of complexity represent superior levels of evolution and development. In this way, evolution represents the blossoming and liberation of the self-organizing and self-evolving potential of the world and of human beings.

The emergent paradigm also posits that many of the elements (e.g., hope, trust, faith, creativity, passion) that construct our reality are nonlinear and complex, and, as such, encumber the use of numbers and formal theory. Thus, whereas the dominant paradigm uses numbers and formal theory to reflect a reality that is supposedly apart from us, the emergent paradigm posits that such a reality is nonexistent. Numbers and formal theory also suggest beginning and ending demarcations, whereas the emergent paradigm posits that such notions miss the variable and complex character of the natural world and human behavior. A related criticism is that the notion that ends follow beginnings reflects a vulgar determinism that precludes the notion that ends and beginnings dwell within each other. Accordingly, proponents of the emergent paradigm posit that the kinds of determinism that characterize the dominant paradigm foreclose on creativity and volition.

It is also believed that social demarcations—such as beginnings and ends, causes and effects—really aid reductionism and obstruct the focus on holism and continuity. Again, the contention is that numbers and formal theory lack the variability, spontaneity, adaptability, and continuity to comprehend a complex and evolving world. The emergent paradigm uses other means to accomplish this task. According to Young, "Qualitative research, employing the richness and passion of human language, can restore to social dynamics the variability, openness, discontinuity and reversibility that aristolean logic, euclidean algebra and newtonian physics strip from social dynamics" (1991, p. 329). In sum, the notion that ends and beginnings dwell within each other is seen as a superior way of understanding the natural world. This notion also spotlights creativity and volition as central features of both the natural world and human behavior.

The emergent paradigm also does away with the duality of order and chaos. Instead, the emergent paradigm posits a dialectical union between order and chaos, which is to say, order resides within chaos and chaos resides within order. As Young explains, "There is never a time in a nonlinear system in which there is no order; never a time in a stable system when there is not disorder. Human agency and human determinism dwell in the same theoretical house" (1992, p. 446). What, then, is chaos? *Chaos is order!* Wallerstein offers an apt description of this order: "[I]t is an unpredicted and unpredictable order; it is a very unstable order; it is very complex order, unreducible to simple equations; and it is order that will always be only approximately measurable" (1992, p. 7). As such, complexity rather than linearity is the defining quality of this order.

High degrees of complexity suggest that potentiality is blossoming and with this comes resiliency. The emergent paradigm asks, "How complex is the order?" Also, "How resilient is the order?" In contrast, the dominant paradigm asks, "Is the order predictable?" "Is the order stable?" The emergent paradigm uses complexity and resiliency to assess predictability. Though both paradigms uphold a notion of determinism, both look at determinism differently. In the emergent paradigm, complexity and resiliency are the features of determinism. In the dominant paradigm, linearity and causality are the defining features. Volition and determinism are both entwined with complexity and resiliency. As Marion succinctly points out, "Behavior is born of simple, deterministic precursors, yet is eminently complex and unpredictable" (1992, p. 170). In other words, the emergent perspective uses complexity to check the certainty of determinism and uses determinism to bring consistency to resiliency. In the end, by employing complexity and resiliency to assess the quality of order (chaos), the emergent paradigm affirms the self-organizing and self-evolving potential of the world.

The emergent paradigm also posits that our humanity is constituted through a dialectical union between potentiality (final causation) and negotiation (efficient causation). Final causation constitutes human action unbridled by social and physical constraint, whereas efficient causation is the effect of context and human artifacts on potentiality. The union comprises an energy and a dissipation component. As Marion explains, "It is the interaction of final and efficient drives—the chaos in life—that makes society and human existence possible. Social behavior is bounded diversity . . . it is finite . . . and stable" (1992, p. 169). Although notions of necessity and stability seem to suggest constraints on potentiality, both are actually necessary to afford predictability and stability and, ultimately, creativity. Efficient causation performs an enabling rather than a constraining function. It enables the development of our humanity by affording communication, meaning, and organizing. It represents the forces that shape and mold. All social constructions and human artifacts, as a matter of fact, represent efficient causation.

Both energy and dissipation are vital to each other. To attain the highest levels of complexity and resiliency and, by that, attain the highest levels of human and collective development, energy levels must exceed dissipation levels. When this occurs, potentiality (final causation) blossoms, heightening creativity and spontaneity. Murray Bookchin offers an apt description of spontaneity, "Spontaneity is behavior, feeling and thought that is free of external restraint, of imposed restriction [efficient causation]. It is self-controlled, internally controlled [final causation], behavior, feeling, and thought, not an uncontrolled effluvium of passion and action" (1980, p. 259). The blossoming of potentiality also represents human and collective actualization.

Complexity, resiliency, creativity, and spontaneity all occur with the releasing of the energy component. The reason this occurs is that all are vital for the survival and well-being of the human condition through periods of disequilibrium. The emergent paradigm views disequilibrium as a constant of evolution and transformation. Disequilibrium represents conflict, diversity, tension, ambiguity. It forces us to find new ways of being by contesting our extant cognitive structures, that is, our extant ways of being. Again, conflict can be dealt with either functionally or dysfunctionally. Disequilibrium commits the human condition to act creatively and spontaneously so as to harness and exploit potential threats. In doing so, resiliency is acquired as disequilibrium catalyzes the blossoming of the self-organizing and self-evolving potential. This naturally (organically) moves us towards higher levels of complexity and resiliency. Whereas disequilibrium acts as a catalyst for evolution and transformation, equilibrium (stability) brings stagnation and devolution and, eventually, death and extinction. Disequilibrium only poses a threat when disproportionately high ratios of efficient causation stifles final causation. In sum, resiliency reflects states with disproportionately high ratios of final causation.

The dialectical union between final and efficient causation gives a theoretical foundation to liberation and oppression. Liberation maximizes the energy component and minimizes the dissipation component; conversely, oppression minimizes the energy component and maximizes the dissipation component. Consequently, liberation demands dismantling the dissipation component. It demands an end to the discursive and material practices that block the evolution of new ways of being. The goal is to end hierarchy. Hierarchy stifles passion, creativity, and spontaneity.

The purest and most productive form of order appears as the dissipation component decreases. This order appears only organically. The emergent paradigm posits that order is of the world. No control or coercion is required. The emergent order that evolves organically facilitates the creative expression of human action through volition rather than coercion. A good analogy is music. To play any kind of music demands knowing the order that governs music. The artist uses this order creatively for self-expression, and the listeners also use the exact order to understand what the artist is expressing. Without any order, the artist lacks the means to transform and manifest what he or she feels. The purest and most productive form of order allows for a limitless amount of creativity. Jazz aptly reflects the limitless, spontaneous creativity that this order affords. Accordingly, the order that governs music, rather than stopping noise (chaos), makes for creative expression.

The dialectical union of final and efficient causation also helps explain why human beings will always resist domination. Neither naturists nor nurturists offer a coherent explanation of this phenomenon. Again, John Brown fighting perilously for the abolition of slavery by no means fits Dawkins and company's explanation of altruism. History, moreover, shows plainly that such behaviors are too universal, even during the heights of the most dehumanizing oppression, to be random as many others suggest. The dialectical union of final and efficient causation also undermines the legitimacy of hierarchy. Hierarchy, a manifestation of efficient causation, blocks the blossoming of our natural strivings for growth, development, creativity, and liberation—that is, final causation. It thwarts the unfolding of our being by undermining our strivings to bring new meaning to bear upon the world. Hierarchy represents the dissipation component. It undercuts our ability to act upon the world by reifying differences. In short, hierarchy functions as coercion. As coercion, hierarchy undermines the open expression of conflict, and this hinders diversity and the evolution of other ways of being. In other words, hierarchy fosters homogeneity and conformity, both of which signal the death of any living system. Without conflict as a catalyst, our strivings to bring forth new meanings are stifled, and thus the possibility of new ways of being is lost.

There is obviously a scholarly fixation with coercion. As I have shown, coercion is a social construction, a product of a paradigm that makes strident distinctions about the natural world. Without the logos that undergirds this paradigm, coercion and all the other attending assumptions and artifacts would presumably be nonexistent. In other words, a paradigm shift is revolutionary.

SUMMARY AND CONCLUSION

History reveals that the cooptive ability of the dominant paradigm is tremendous. It is now evident that a lot of the emergent paradigm has already been successfully coopted. The notion that order that arises organically is superior to that which is imposed is now making for best-selling management books. Management and business schools label the emergent paradigm revolutionary. It makes for new management, leadership, marketing, and manufacturing techniques. But the problem with cooptation is always what goes uninterrogated. What is going uninterrogated with the cooptation now occurring is the hegemony of capital/labor relations. Propositions of the emergent paradigm are cast apart from the context that is essential to understand that this worldview undermines everything *of* the dominant paradigm.

Cooptation defangs the emergent paradigm. It reduces the emergent worldview to an emergent perspective. It is stripped of that which makes for a paradigm shift—a new ontology, new ways of being and experiencing the world. It is never realized that the emergent worldview brings forth new conceptualizations of our relations to the world and each other. Certainly, as a result of cooptation, the dominant paradigm will boast of new truths and other alterations, and this will probably prolong the day of reckoning. Its consciousness, however, can never be changed, and this is what threatens to eventually damn us all. Its debilitating effects on our humanity are real. Its problems are structural. The consciousness that the emergent paradigm engenders clashes with everything *of* the dominant paradigm. Without a doubt the end of domination and coercion will mean the end of the status quo.

A deep distrust and suspicion of human beings and the world makes for a fixation with complex, rigid, and hierarchical structures. It fosters the belief that structures end anarchy and chaos. Order is seen as an artifact of control. In these ways, the dominant paradigm engenders the belief that the world is dependent on human beings for order. Yet, on the other hand, the dominant paradigm is premised on the notion that the world is orderly. Evidently, the matter is contradictory. Yet a belief that the world is dependent on human beings for order legitimizes the dominant paradigm.

The emergent paradigm releases us from our deep distrust and suspicion of the world. It gives us a vista to look at human beings and the world anew. The notion of potentiality is a fecund theoretical proposition. The notion of order versus that of law is also fecund. As Evelyn Fox Keller explains, "The concept of order, wider than law and free from its coercive, hierarchical, and centralizing implications, has the potential to expand our conception of science. Order is a category comprising patterns of organization that can be spontaneous, self-generated, or externally imposed; it is a larger category than law precisely to the extent that law implies external constraint" (1985, p. 132). Our next task is to identify the ways of being that will make for the blossoming of this potentiality. Certainly, coercion and hierarchy will have to go. The emergent paradigm posits that this is a world of relationships. Human beings and the world are constituted relationally. Consequently, discursive and material practices that accent relationships rather than structures are required. Our preoccupation with structures undermines our ability to establish deep and meaningful human relations. The result is dysfunctionality. Ultimately, what is required is a new consciousness of the world rather than merely a new worldview or perspective or new management philosophy.

4

The Nature of Nonhierarchical Relations

We focus now on the mechanics of nonhierarchical ways of being. Again, rather than merely an arrangement of differences, hierarchy is a social arrangement based on coercion, domination, and subordination. It is an artifact of *man*. It is, specifically, a social construction dependent on the reification of stratified differences and dysfunctional meaning creation practices that suppress the open expression of conflict. Supposedly, the open expression of conflict threatens social devolution and death. In this way, hierarchy undercuts the blossoming of our existential and spiritual strivings. It undercuts the possibility of liberation. Simply put, the discursive and material practices that sustain hierarchy thwart our moral, existential, and spiritual strivings.

The result of hierarchy is moral minimalism. This secularization of morality is epitomized by looking to apes, chimpanzees, monkeys, bonobos, and other animals for our moral codes. Foundational to moral minimalism is the notion that human beings are amoral and naturally aexistential and aspiritual. This view suggests that human beings must be forcibly equipped with moral codes. Moral minimalism stresses selfishness and autonomy. It assumes that good moral behavior is foremost about what is good for oneself. It posits no existential relation between community and being. All human relations are characterized essentially as manipulative and exploitative. I strongly disagree with this perspective. To argue for a different view, I focus on the discursive and material practices that nurture the blossoming of our existential and strivings and thereby foster human and collective development. My goal is to show that such practices will end hierarchy and coercion.

INTRINSIC FORCES

Past research provides good descriptions of our existential and spiritual strivings. The research by Jack Gibb is compelling for numerous reasons. It is especially so given the attributes of the study, specifically the long duration of data collection in both laboratory and field contexts, and the overt political neutrality. Gibb (1964) found support for the thesis that four modal concerns—acceptance, data-flow, goal, control—arise from all social interactions. The notion of acceptance deals with the formation of trust and reduction of fear of self and others. The data-flow concept deals with the flow of feeling, perceptual data, and spontaneity. The goal concept focuses on the integration of motivations to afford problem-solving and decision-making. Finally, the control concept concerns regulatory mechanisms for coordination and organization. Gibb found that "These concerns generate *intrinsic forces* that reduce the concerns and produce personal growth and development" (p. 280, emphasis added). Unfortunately, Gibb never elaborated on the exact nature of those intrinsic forces.

However, according to Gibb, "Growth in each dimension [concern] is contingent upon growth in each of the dimensions higher in the hierarchy [acceptance concern is first]. Each factor in the hierarchy provides a pace-setting or boundary function for the factors lower in the hierarchy" (1964, p. 283). Gibb consistently found that after a minimum amount of training to aid trust formation, growth quickly and organically occurred throughout all the concerns. He explains, "We found that groups tended to take over direction of their own processes and to move more quickly towards growth when given greatest freedom and least prescribed structure" (p. 301).

Gibb never discusses hierarchy specifically. He theorizes about leaderless collectives. But particularly striking from among his findings is how hierarchy disappears spontaneously and concurrently as human beings and collectives grow and develop. In other words, transformation and development appear as domination and subordination disappear. The features of growth and development that Gibb describes are diversity, nonconformity, open expression of feeling and conflict, cooperation, reduced apathy, creativity, decreased need for organizational structures, and consensus decision-making. On the other hand, underdevelopment is characterized by apathy, competition, fear, distrust, manipulation, and dependency. It reflects a deep fear of the world.

Gibb's observations point to a negative correlation between hierarchy and growth, development, transformation. Hierarchy undermines the ceaseless self-organizing and self-evolving potential of human beings and human collectives. It blocks the attainment of superior levels of organization by suppressing our natural striving to bring meaning to bear upon the world. Reproduction is achieved at the cost of creation. It maintains this condition through fear and through our own unwillingness to confront the world genuinely and transparently. Hierarchy sacrifices deep and meaningful relationships for rigid and complex structures. It is through the forging of deep and meaningful human relation that our striving for meaning is fully realized. Conversely, hierarchy dehumanizes human beings by thwarting relationships and suppressing meaning creation. About the relation between hierarchy and dysfunctionality, Larry Spence writes:

> Because of the cognitive damage required for adaptation to the conditions of hierarchies, knowledge appears to be harmful to individuals within such organizations. They behave much as do persons suffering from temporary or permanent disabilities of the brain or other organs who defend themselves from the catastrophic confrontation with their disability. Defenses such as a retreat, apathy, and denial are biologically functional in hierarchical situations but they have dangerous political implications. Harmful and damaging social contexts are likely to lead to censored aspirations and obstacles against awareness rather than to critical assessments and needed reforms. The apathy, dogmatism, resistance to change, and ignorance attributed to human nature are more the result of the formation of narrow cognitive structures under the survival demands of specific social contexts than the result of any inherent propensities of the specifies. Organizational contexts characterized by dissembling or disguise

of crucial features, overrepetition of behavioral patterns, and
overmotivation or frustration result in functional brain damage.
(1978, p. 8)

Gibb's observations aptly showcase the fecundity of human
potentiality and the natural propensity of this potential to unfold and
blossom organically. In this way, his observations compellingly coun-
terpoints the view of human beings posited by Dawkins, Wilson, and
company. What makes this contradiction especially compelling is
that Gibb's observations are derived from the actual study of human
beings. Neither Richard Dawkins nor E. O. Wilson can make this
claim.

Gibb's observations also debunk Gaylin and Jennings' contention that market forces produce superior social order. The symmetry of the features of growth and development that Gibb observes
suggests that human beings have a natural propensity for human and
collective development. In addition, the kinds of coercion that Gaylin
and Jennings deem necessary are actually debilitating rather than
merely unnecessary. Coercion, as Gibb's observations compellingly
show, undercuts our natural strivings for transformation and development. It blocks the evolution of ways of being that directly contest
the legitimacy of the status quo. In this way, Gibb's observations
explicitly reveal that coercion is an artifact of dysfunctionality rather
than functionality. Consequently, rather than a catalyst of life, as
Dawkins, Wilson, and company vociferously contend, competition is
an artifact of social devolution. Competition reflects dysfunctionality.
It thwarts the blossoming of our existential and spiritual strivings,
thus blocking the development of our moral capacity. Our moral
capacity is entwined with our functionality.

The human striving for transparency reveals a lot about
being human and about our propensity or predisposition to a certain
kind of human relations. I am by no means calling for a normative
theory of transparency. To suggest that transparency is the beginning
and end of liberation delegitimizes the tremendous complexity that
constitutes human action. Human action is rational and nonrational,
linear and nonlinear, selfish and unselfish, cultural and psychological, conscious and unconscious, and so forth. Throughout this project
I have argued that the complexity of human action undermines the
claim that human action is predominantly shaped by a fixed set of
drives, states, natures, or the like. It would be theoretical hypocrisy
to suggest now that human action revolves around a need to be
transparent, or to call for a normative theory of transparency.

The need or striving for transparency reveals that human beings have a natural aversion to deception. *We would prefer to be open to the world.* Transparency rather than deception is the natural predisposition of human beings. This proclivity for transparency contradicts the view that hierarchy is our natural condition. It reveals, rather, our predisposition to nonhierarchical ways of being. Moreover, this proclivity for transparency is a vital element in the foundation of nonhierarchical human relations. It also gives an existential origin to nonhierarchical relations. In other words, the origin of nonhierarchical relations transcends our social and material worlds. The proclivity toward transparency shows that all human beings are equipped—however meagerly or imperfectly—with the motivation and ability to form nonhierarchical human relations. Finally, our proclivity for transparency gives us a moral ground that also transcends our social and material worlds. Regardless of the endless arguments that proponents of hierarchy now offer, the fact is that the effects of hierarchy—specifically deception—are real and debilitating. The suppression of transparency is fundamentally an unnatural condition. Purely from the standpoint of human physiology, hierarchy harms life. If hierarchy is such a good and natural arrangement, as proponents now claim, what explains this debilitating effect? In other words, proponents claim that the forces of natural selection affirm life, and that hierarchy—by supposedly being the vital mechanism that affords evolution—is born of this ambition. However, the research compellingly show that transparency—the antithesis of hierarchy—is what actually affirms life.

CONFLICT AND COMPETITION

Those who apply natural selection theory to human behavior have successfully propagated the notion that competition is the origin of all conflict. The result is that competition is commonly conflated with conflict. In fact, most proponents of natural selection theory usually make no distinction between conflict and competition. In *Darwin's Dangerous Idea*, Daniel Dennett never evens mentions conflict. Dennett also contends that communication is an artifact of competition/conflict. Our capacity for communication supposedly evolved purely for mediating conflict. It is a secular creation. In this view, no existential relation exists between conflict (functional) and human and collective development. Moreover, the perspective admits no relation between different kinds of conflict and the communication practices that make for either functional or dysfunctional conflict. Again, Dennett believes that conflict is constant and set by the forces of nature.

It is also common to view competition as regulated conflict. Competition is supposedly a continuous struggle for mutually desired goals characterized by agreed upon rules and norms that prohibit coercion or the forceful removal of participants. Scarcity is also common to definitions of competition. According to Friedsam, "Competition is that form of interaction which involves a struggle for goals which are scarce; the interaction is normatively regulated, may be direct or indirect, personal or impersonal, and tends to exclude the use of violence" (1964, p. 118). Conflict, on the other hand, is supposedly about opposition of goals, beliefs, values, needs, and so forth. Angell writes, "Although conflict and competition have in common the fact of struggle, they differ in the main objective of struggle—for conflict, it is defeat of the opponent; for competition, it is to appropriate a scarce resource" (1965, p. 113). Clinton Fink (1968) calls for a broad definition of social conflict that embraces both scarcity and incompatibility. According to Linda Putnam and Marshall Scott Poole, both Professors of Communication at Texas A & M University, conflict is "the interaction of interdependent people who perceive opposition of goals, and values, and who see the other party as potentially interfering with the realization of these goals" (1987, p. 552). David Mortensen posits:

> Human conflicts are . . . products of a confluence of animalistic urge and ecological necessity sustained by two or more sources at the same time. From a communicative standpoint, conflicts may be viewed as expressed struggles over the distribution of scarce resources—material, economic, and symbolic. Conflicts redefine and thereby alter communal ties insofar as they facilitate the redistribution (or reapportionment) of whatever it is that humans may lack but nonetheless value. This in turn means that to create conflict one must be able to resist or challenge some aspect of the existing order. Those who lack shelter and nourishment are apt to be too weak or helpless to be able to put up a good verbal fight. (1991, p. 276)

The legacy of tying conflict with competition is a deep distrust and suspicion of conflict. The result is a discursive predisposition to suppressing conflict. We fear that conflict threatens stability.

Indeed, stability is commonly seen as the negation of conflict. However, most discussions of competition and conflict miss the human element. Incompatibility and scarcity are social constructions; both are artifacts of meaning creation processes; both reflect the communication that frames the nature of social interaction. The preceding views also miss the cultural component of conflict and competition. Different cultural contexts make for different understandings of and predispositions to conflict. Sahlins put the matter the following way:

> What is reproduced in human cultural orders is not human beings qua human beings *but the system of social groups, categories, and relations in which they live.* . . . The reason why human social behavior is not organized by the individual maximization of genetic interest is that human beings are not socially defined by their organic qualities but in terms of symbolic attributes; and a symbol is precisely a meaningful value . . . which cannot be determined by the physical properties of that which it refers. (1976, pp. 60-61; emphasis in original)

We have already seen that proponents of natural selection theory foster the notion that our definition of conflict is set by the forces of nature. In other words, the occurrence and outcomes of conflict are completely and rigidly determined by objective circumstances (Deutsch, 1969). However, situations that are framed competitively can just as well be framed cooperatively. Cox, Lobel, and McLeod (1991) show this plainly. Moreover, scarcity must be created to sustain competition. This is achieved through a variety of means. It is, foremost, achieved through the *illusion of scarcity*. We sustain this illusion by engendering a constant fear of others. In sum, scarcity is a discursive creation. We can end competition by developing discursive and material practices that accent unselfishness rather than selfishness.

Most discussions of competition and conflict also miss the distinction between functional and dysfunctional conflict (Nicotera, 1993; Putnam & Poole, 1987; Witteman, 1991). The distinction is by no means arbitrary. It reflects the kinds of discursive and nondiscursive practices that produce conflict. Critical evaluation of ideas, idea generation, discussion of goals, outcome orientation, and flexibility are key features that distinguish functional and dysfunctional conflict (Witteman, 1991). Functional and dysfunctional conflict really reflect different orientations. The latter reflects a deep distrust and suspicion of our humanity. It is affective, combative, and generally destructive.

Dysfunctional conflict discourages open discussion of collective goals through deception and coercion. Conflict is seen as the precursor to chaos and anarchy. Dysfunctional conflict is characterized by fear, suspicion, and deception. It reeks with hostility. The objective is to end and suppress conflict. In circumscribing and suppressing conflict, however, certain views and ways of being are privileged. Simply put, dysfunctional conflict suppresses diversity and engenders domination. Conversely, diversity is an artifact of the open expression of conflict. It reflects the blossoming of our existential and spiritual strivings. It thrives with the end of hierarchy.

Functional conflict is characterized by transparency and openness. It reflects a willingness to confront the world genuinely. It is also characterized by empathy and unselfishness. Conflict is negotiated through persuasion rather than coercion. Negotiators seek common ground and stress good will. Morton Deutsch writes that "It [functional conflict] prevents stagnation, it stimulates interest and curiosity, it is the medium through which problems can be aired and solutions arrived at; it is the root of personal and social change" (1969, p. 17). According to Robert Baruch Bush and Joseph Folger, authors of *The Promise of Mediation*:

> A conflict confronts each party with a challenge, a difficulty or adversity to be grappled with. This challenge presents parties with the opportunity to clarify for themselves their needs and values, what causes them dissatisfaction and satisfaction. It also gives them the chance to discover and strengthen their own resources for addressing both substantive concerns and relational issues. In short, conflict affords people the opportunity to develop and exercise both self-determination and self-reliance. Moreover, the emergence of conflict confronts each party with a differently situated other who holds a contrary viewpoint. This encounter presents each party with an opportunity for acknowledging the perspectives of others. It gives the individual the chance to feel and express some degree of understanding and concern for another, despite diversity and disagreement. Conflict thus gives people the occasion to develop and exercise respect and consideration of others. In sum, conflicts embody valuable opportunities for both dimensions of moral growth, perhaps to a greater degree than most other human experiences. (1994, p. 82)

Research shows that transparency correlates with the fairness of outcomes, specifically win/win outcomes (e.g., Witteman, 1991). With high levels of openness all persons know what constitutes fair and equitable outcomes. In other words, openness undercuts members' ability to mask selfish ambitions. In this way, high levels of openness block domination and subordination. The result is that high levels of openness make for cooperation rather than competition. Finally, whereas competition engenders rigidity, cooperation engenders flexibility. Witteman describes flexibility as both a willingness and an ability to adjust perceptually and behaviorally to new conflict situations. Flexibility characterizes functional conflict. The commitment to win/win outcomes encourages flexibility. Without the weapon of manipulation—which, again, openness takes away— the ability of members to attain selfish outcomes becomes difficult. In addition, openness fosters high levels of warmth, security, attraction, commitment, and trust, all of which engender flexibility (Witteman, 1991). Flexibility represents the ebb and flow of life. It manifests the capacity of conflict to exercise our striving for deep and meaningful relations. Robert Baruch Bush and Joseph Folger posit:

> Responding to conflicts productively means utilizing the opportunities they present to change and transform the parties as human beings. It means encouraging and helping the parties to use the conflict to realize and actualize their inherent capacities both for strength of self and for relating to others. It means bringing out the intrinsic goodness that lies within the parties as human beings. If this is done, then the response to conflict itself helps transform individuals from fearful, defensive, or self-centered beings into confident, responsive, and caring ones, ultimately transforming society as well. (1994, pp. 82-83)

To move beyond popular understandings of conflict toward the view expressed above demands a new set of assumptions. We need new definitions of conflict. A definition of conflict that rests on the presupposition that human beings have existential and spiritual strivings for deep and meaningful relations allows us to view conflict as any real or perceived threat to our cognitive, sensual, and spiritual stability. This emergent definition entwines conflict with human and collective development. It gives conflict an existential and spiritual foundation—an ethics that is existentially and spiritually based. Conflict is a life catalyst. By disturbing our cognitive, sensual, and spiritual stability, conflict forces us to look at the world anew, thus making for the entry of new ways of being and experiencing the world. Without conflict, this possibility would be nonexistent. In other words, conflict is a vital element of growth and development.

In fact, meaningful development is impossible without conflict. Conflict potentially blocks the reifying of meanings and, by that, the evolution of rigid structures. In this way, functional conflict makes for the creation of new meanings and new perspectives, both of which are vital for human and collective development. Conversely, dysfunctional conflict and the ways of being that engender such conflict are, besides being dysfunctional, unethical. The reason is that dysfunctional conflict undercuts the blossoming of our existential and spiritual strivings. It reduces human beings to beasts.

Competition also reduces human beings to beasts. It thwarts human and collective development by engendering human relations laden with distrust, suspicion, and selfishness. It blocks the formation of discursive openness by reifying the belief that openness will ultimately make for our own exploitation and subjugation. Deception becomes habitual behavior so as to mask our real thoughts and motives. There is correspondingly a constant fear of being duped. In short, our discursive and material practices are laden with distrust and suspicion. All of this springs from our distrust and suspicion of our own humanity. Competition, like dysfunctional conflict, is an artifact of this distrust and suspicion. Competition undermines the full development of our moral capacity. It further engenders distrust, suspicion, and fear, as win/win outcomes are structurally unattainable. In this way, competition actually exacerbates our distrust and suspicion of others by imposing a discursive reward orientation that is divisive and unequal. By engendering fear, distrust, and selfishness, competition blocks the evolution of trust. Conversely, competition undercuts the evolution of meaningful levels of openness, which is vital for the evolution of equality and cooperation. In this way, competition adversely affects human and collective development.

TRANSPARENCY AND COOPERATION

What is emerging so far are complex and naturally binding relationships among such notions as equality, diversity, openness, security, affiliation, trust, and cooperation. The symmetry of the arrangements reflects something that Erich Fromm once said about liberation:

> It must be clearly understood, though, that freedom is not lais-sez-faire and arbitrariness. Human beings have a specific struc-

ture—like any other species—and can grow only in terms of this structure. Freedom does not mean freedom *from* all guiding principles. It means the freedom *to grow* according to the laws of the structure of human existence . . . . It means obedience to the laws that govern optimal human development. (1976, p. 80; emphasis in original)

Human beings possess a need for transparency. Fulfilling this need is vital for both human and collective development. In *Self-Disclosure: An Experimental Analysis of The Transparent Self*, Sydney Jourard writes:

Transparency . . . is a multifaceted mode of being—it calls for a courage and a willingness to let the world be what it is, to let the other be who he is, and to let oneself be who one is. It calls as well for a commitment to truth, as it changeably presents itself. It calls for a readiness to suspend concepts and beliefs about self, others, and [the] world, and to perceive what is. It calls for a willingness to suspend imagination, wish, and fantasy, a readiness to inform and revise concepts with fresh inputs of perception. That it calls for courage to disclose oneself to the world is self-evident. (1971, p. 182)

Much research points to a relationship between levels of transparency and mental health (Blotchy, Carscanddon, & Grandmaison, 1983; Garcia & Geisler, 1988; Greenberg & Stone, 1992; Pennebaker & Beall, 1986; Stiles, Shuster, & Harrigan, 1992). Obstructing this propensity by suppressing thoughts, feelings, and behaviors is destructive. The research also shows that transparency correlates with relationship development (e.g., Chelune, 1989; Hansen & Schuldt, 1984; Prager, 1986; Tolstedt & Stokes, 1984). In reality, this need for transparency is a manifestation of final causation. Retribution and social punishment, on the other hand, represent efficient causation. In other words, this need for transparency represents an existential and spiritual striving. Transparency affirms life. It also fulfills our capacity to act morally and ethically. Audre Lorde writes, "The need for sharing deep feelings is a human need. . . . To refuse to be conscious of what we are feeling at any time, however comfortable that might seem, is to deny a large part of the experience, and to allow ourselves to be reduced to the . . . abused, and the absurd" (1984, pp. 58-59). In sum, discursive and material practices that engender deception rather than transparency are unethical.

Transparency also catalyzes trust. Trust is arguably the most vital element of human and collective development. Consequently, as a result of ending deception, the evolution of transparency blocks manipulation. The end of deception is vital for the possibility of human and collective development. According to Audre Lorde, "As we begin to recognize our deepest feelings, we begin to give up, of necessity, being satisfied with suffering and self-negation, and with the numbness which so often seems like their only alternative in our society. Our acts of oppression become integral with self, motivated and empowered from within" (1984, p. 58).

Peter Kropotkin recognized over a century ago that the origins of cooperation are existential. He deserves credit for bringing a tremendous body of scholarship to bear on the thesis that cooperation rather than competition is the natural order of things. He sought to develop a system of ethics that was consistent with this thesis. With such a system, he believed, humanity could avoid the tyranny of superstition and mysticism. He also saw competition responsible for human degradation and a threat to the future well-being of humanity. He believed that the evolution of cooperation reflects the blossoming of all of our being. According to Kropotkin:

> [T]he instinct of self-preservation is by no means sufficient to account for all the strivings of man [sic]. . . . Side by side with the instinct of self-preservation there exists in us another instinct: the striving toward a more intensive, and varied life, toward widening its limits beyond the realm of self-preservation. Life is not limited to nutrition, it demands mental fecundity and spiritual activity rich in impressions, feelings, and manifestations of will. (1992, p. 326)

Kropotkin argued that hierarchy is an artifact of social devolution. He held that hierarchy encumbers our potentiality by encouraging competition through the promotion of selfishness. He warned again and again of the dangers of encumbering of our existential strivings: "Like the need [for] food, shelter . . . these instincts are self-preservation instincts. Of course, they may sometimes be weakened under the influence of certain circumstances, and we know many cases when the power of these instincts is relaxed, for one reason or the other . . . the group . . . begins to fail in the struggle for life; it moves towards its decay" (p. 31). Kropotkin also theorized that equality and cooperation were artifacts of collective development. He also saw the relation between equality and collective development as an ethical statement about the world. According to Kropotkin:

The fundamental faculty of human reason is . . . *the conception of justice*. . . . There is, and there can be, no other rule that may become the universal criterion judging human acts. And what is more, this criterion is recognized, not fully, but to a considerable extent, by other thinking human beings . . . [and] by many social animals. It is impossible to explain this faculty of our reason in any other way than in connection with the progressive development, i.e., the *evolution*, of man and the animal world in general. If this is true, it is impossible to deny that the principal endeavor of man is his striving for personal happiness in the broadest sense of that word. (1992, p. 221; emphasis in original)

Kropotkin also posits:

The moral element in man needs, therefore, no coercion, no compulsory obligation, no sanction from above; it develops in us by virtue of the very need of man to live a full, intensive, productive life. Man is not content with ordinary commonplace existence; he seeks the opportunity to extend its limits, to accelerate its tempo, to fill it with varied impressions and emotional experiences. And as long he feels in himself the ability to attain this end he will not wait for any coercion or command from without. (p. 323)

Kropotkin considered equality as both an aspiration and an artifact of human relations that reflect the full richness of human expression and experiences. In this way, he understood that compassion is integral to collective development. In *Mutual Aid*, he writes, "Compassion is a necessary outcome of social life. But compassion also means a considerable advance in general intelligence and sensibility. It is the first step towards the development of higher moral sentiments. It is, in turn, a powerful factor of further evolution" (p. 60). Evidently, Kropotkin also understood that moving equality from the realm of the political to that of the existential and spiritual redefines our common understandings of the good society.

The equality that comes with the evolution of cooperation is also about diversity. It bespeaks the endless potentiality of all human beings. It releases us from predetermined groupings and the consequences of those groupings. Any kind of categorization or predetermination circumscribes our humanity to human artifacts rather than the consciousness of the world. In other words, predetermined groupings represent efficient causation. In this way, the diversity that emerges through cooperation is really about restoring complexity to our humanity and human relations; accenting the diversity and richness of our humanity; realizing that this diversity and richness are vital to the well-being of any society; acknowledging the potential and fecundity of our humanity; and recognizing the ability of human beings to grow, develop, and blossom. In sum, the equality that comes with the evolution of cooperation is existentially entwined with our diversity, complexity, and potentiality. In this way, equality, rather than merely a political and cultural artifact, actually characterizes the nature of our moral, existential, and spiritual strivings. It bespeaks an aspiration of human beings to find new levels of being. It challenges, moreover, the popular belief that human beings are amoral, aexistential, and aspiritual.

Equality is entwined with the evolution of trust, empathy, unselfishness, and compassion. It emerges organically with the end of domination. By contrast, a coerced equality, regardless of however benevolent the ambition, is no equality at all. It is merely conformity. The quest to attain this kind of uniform equality makes for the reification of processes and practices that subordinate the existential and spiritual needs of members to the secular demands of the collective. What emerges is an unnecessary tension between what is best for members compared to what is best for the collective. In this way, conformity and uniformity make for an *ideology of deviancy* that further legitimizes our distrust and suspicion of our humanity and the necessity of hierarchy.

The quest to attain equality through conformity and uniformity ultimately leads to the evolution and reification of structures and processes that strive to make group members uniformly equal. The result is homogeneity rather than equality. But anything other than a full respect for differences is a violation of human dignity. Of course, what represents a violation of human dignity is discursive and material practices that obstruct the evolution of our existential and spiritual strivings. To look at equality as merely about limiting differences is to mask the structures and processes—such as hierarchy—that thwart our becoming fully human and truly threaten the blossoming of differences. This approach to equality merely encourages the reification of secular differences (such as race, gender, ethnicity), and shifts the focus away from matters of moral development. It ultimately makes for a narrow conception of human dignity.

Dorothy Lee provides a compellingly analysis of the relation between the blossoming of diversity and the negation of coercion. Lee found that many native groups were without discursive practices that afford comparison and coercion. She concludes that both are really social constructions:

In the Western world, we have in our system of thought, notions and attitudes which predispose us to evaluation in terms of inequality. Assessment and even apprehension of objects of knowledge in terms of comparison, is fundamental to our thinking. We know that a thing is good because we recognize it *as good as or better than*; we know that an infant is tall or slow only when we know his [sic] age, that is, when we can compare him with the infants in his age-group. We define according to similarities and dissimilarities, according to qualities which can be analyzed and abstracted out of the field of consideration [It is adjectives that afford comparison]. (1987, p. 42; emphasis in original)

Lee observes that, by contrast, the Trobianders of the South Pacific are devoid of discursive practices that allow for comparisons:

This language offers no mechanism for comparison; it offers instead a large number of terms for what would be for us the same object with varying degrees of the same quality. For instance, the yam of appropriate ripeness for harvesting is termed a *taytu*, but for the not-quite-ripe and the over-ripe there are completely different terms. The difference is not of degree; it is an aspect of uniqueness. People desire to be good (or rather good-gardeners); not *better than*. . . . Neither he [sic] nor others made a practice of evaluating his work against a comparative standard of achievement or expectation. Striving was not for equality nor for superiority; it was for the enhancement of uniqueness. (pp. 42-43; emphasis in original)

Lee also reports on the Wintu Indians of California, who also are without any "hierarchy conferring differential respect and privilege." Consequently, coercion is nonexistent. According to Lee:

The relationship of coordination, the democracy of the culture, is implemented throughout the grammar of the language. The verbal suffixes which we would automatically see as transitivizers, express instead the relationship of coordination or sharing or cooperation; to do to, is rendered in Wintu as: to do *with*, or to share an experience with. (pp. 43-44; emphasis in original)

Lee posits that many native groups focus on the affirmation of uniqueness—rather than on equality—through various discursive and material practices. Such practices are foremost about allowing each person to develop without coercion. Lee contends that the negation of both comparison and coercion, and the overwhelming focus on uniqueness, nurtures mutual helpfulness rather than competition. The result, she claims, is an understanding of civility and decency that surpasses many extant ones.

The point is that there is a moral calculus embedded within the relation between transparency and human and collective development. The relation shows compellingly that the world is moral. It also offers a compelling description of the moral order that resides within our potentiality.

MORAL MINIMALISM

The dominant notion of morality can best be described as a kind of moral minimalism. The goal is to equip citizens coercively with moral codes. A lot of the quarrel is about who should do the equipping. Many favor market institutions, and others favor family, religious, or educational institutions. The goal is to strip human behavior of all complexity and diversity. It is believed that complexity and diversity can potentially upset the control and stability required for the making of the good society. In *Democracy and Moral Development*, David Norton writes:

> By ontologizing self-interest economically, modernity narrowed human aspirations to suit the emerging opportunities. Moral minimalism resulted from the eradication from modern consciousness of the recognition of higher levels of moral development. It also resulted from the modern constriction of morality to but a sector of life. . . . The effect of modern moral minimalism is to afford to moral life little space for the aspiration that is a definitive human trait; it is a small room with a low ceiling and not much of a view. A telling consequence of this has been to redirect human aspirations away from the confines of morality and toward the apparently limitless horizons afforded by the laboratory and market. (1991, pp. 40-41)

Moral minimalism represents a negation of us as moral beings. It depicts us as having no existential moral calculus. As a result, theorists have no qualms about looking to apes, bonobos, and chimpanzees for moral direction. The result is human relations laden with coercion but devoid of any opportunity for meaningful moral development (i.e., human development) and a society that increasingly resorts to coercion to attain anything remotely resembling human decency. Simply put, moral minimalism engenders social devolution. In this way, liberation without moral development leads to promiscuity.

To end moral minimalism demands releasing ourselves of conceptions of our humanity that are laden with fear, suspicion, and distrust. We need a conception that highlights our existential and spiritual attributes and, as a result, connects moral development with the forging of deep and meaningful relations. This kind of moral development can only be found through our proclivity and capacity to bring meaning to bear on the world. We can begin by looking at how meaning is being brought to bear on the world. This demands consideration of the vibrancy of the meaning creation process. Is the process allowing for new and different meanings? Is the process open to all participants, and equally so? Is the process affirming the possibility of new meanings, thereby affirming all participants? Is the process devoid of punishment and retribution? Moreover, are discursive prisms transparent? In other words, are our beliefs, values, assumptions, and truths being constantly challenged and scrutinized?

No meaning creation can occur without a significant element of unselfishness. In fact, communication as meaning construction and negotiation shows unselfishness as something existential. The most elemental kind of unselfishness is agreement on what symbols mean. In this way, communication binds us to each other; it checks selfishness. Moreover, according to Arthur Shulman:

> [T]he communication process incorporates the meaning generation process, but in a particular way. The communication process incorporates more than one reader and this adds complexity to the meaning generation process. It is the way in which these people are in relation with each other that provides the basis for our conception of communication. Moreover, this process not only creates its own internal structure but also sets its own boundaries. Communication, as an autopoietic process . . . is self-generating, structure-creating, and boundary setting. In acting in this process we find ourselves in a rather more difficult place than conventionally proposed. Communication activity is not only self-generating, it is also self-specifying. (1996, p. 368)

In a compelling essay on the ethics of communication, Lee Thayer makes a poignant observation:

Out of fear of freedom and out of the insecurity of incompetence and out of guilt of having failed themselves, people cluster around static communication realities as chilled men cluster about a fire. They cluster around fixed beliefs and immutable ideologies to provide mutual assurance through emotional blackmail, and to avoid the uncertain risks of thinking for themselves. Ideally, human societies might have set us free from an unconscious world so that we might be all that we could be in a conscious world. But unable to live with himself in a world in which the choice of what could be is his, man [sic] lives without himself in and through others, in a world in which he no longer has to feel responsible for either the choice or its consequences. He imprisons himself in collective ideologies and beliefs and conventional wisdom, in order to be free of any individual responsibility for them. (1973, p. 140)

We must recognize our moral obligation to ourselves and to each other. Refusing to accept such a responsibility for our ways of being is unethical. It bespeaks a lack of moral development. That our communication behavior bears directly on the humanity of others suggests that the transactional nature of our connection to each other is morally and ethically laden.

To block the evolution of new meanings is to undercut the possibility of both new ways of being and experiencing the world. This blocking represents the negation of creation—a suppressing of the natural order of the world. As Thayer explains, "What we do know is that what preserves a social institution does not necessarily enlarge or enrich or fulfill human potential. What we do know is that what is in the best self-interests of individuals or of people in general is not necessarily preservative of certain social institutions" (1973, p. 137). In short, our proclivity is creation rather than reproduction. Creation involves our engaging the world and other human beings. It represents an affirmation of the potentiality of the world and of human beings.

What deep and meaningful relations reflect most is unselfishness. This unselfishness is vital for the possibility of new meanings. Unselfishness includes affirmation, trust, empathy, compassion, tenderness, and kindness. It is a recursive artifact of both human and relational development.

The relation between ambiguity and cognitive stability also needs to be understood dialectically. Nothing is existentially wrong with ambiguity. Ambiguity organically catalyzes our proclivity for meaning, which makes for the blossoming of our existential and spiritual strivings. Ambiguity makes for new meanings, and, as a result, new ways of being and experiencing the world. Accordingly, without ambiguity, our ability to become fully human would be nonexistent. What also needs to be noted is that ambiguity is ubiquitous. Cognitive stability devoid of ambiguity is humanly unattainable. The problem is with our relation to ambiguity. A deep fear of ambiguity engenders subordination. It reflects a fear of new meanings and new ways of being and experiencing the world. There is a fear to risk life. In fear, people focus on sustaining the status quo. Reproduction rather than creation is the norm. In this regard, our fixation is with structures rather than relationships. Our aim is to control the actions of others so as to maintain a reality that matches our own selfish ambitions and concerns. The cruelty of our domination correlates with our fear of ambiguity. Accordingly, manipulation, subordination, and domination are all artifacts of a relation to ambiguity characterized by fear and suspicion.

A consciousness that embraces ambiguity engenders new meanings and new ways of being. Ambiguity represents an opportunity to transcend the present. We must create a context that tenderly nurtures our natural aversion to ambiguity. Such a context affirms human beings as moral, existential, and spiritual beings. In this way, a context that embraces ambiguity gives us the necessary nurturing and support to reach for new meanings by allowing us to be transparent to the world and each other. In addition, a context that embraces ambiguity engenders the unselfishness that is vital for the creation of new meanings. It engenders discursive openness. The goal is to establish communion with the world and each other.

SUMMARY AND CONCLUSION

I aim to move the focus away from our origins to our potential. I have never said that human beings are potentially perfect or without any proclivity for evil. Instead, I have said that proponents of such views have yet to offer compelling support. I have pointed out the many flaws that prominent arguments about the nature of our humanity contain. The fact that such flaws exist releases us just enough from such views to consider different conceptions of being human. I have sought to exploit this opportunity. Moreover, I contend that a focus on origins makes for dysfunctional politics. It engenders dread and fear, fatalism and nihilism. It blocks scrutiny of the status quo. It releases us from our responsibility to each other. It legitimizes dysfunctional ways of being.

We can focus on the potential of being human without pre-supposing that human beings are perfectly good. In addition, though I contend that meaning creation and other strivings distinguish human beings from animals, a strident distinction is unnecessary. We will never exactly know our origins. Further, a distinction can be made without positing a hierarchy between human beings and animals. Nonetheless, our existential and spiritual strivings represent a real enough distinction to demand that researchers who wish to make strident claims about human beings—especially when such claims shape social/political policy—study human beings rather than chimpanzees, monkeys, bonobos, and rodents. I have focused on the discursive and material practices that undercut our existential and spiritual strivings. Such undercutting thwarts the development of our moral development. Only through the development of deep and meaningful relations is our moral capacity realized. In sum, our moral development is entwined with the blossoming of our existential and spiritual strivings.

We may eventually find that human beings are hopelessly flawed. Our homicidal leanings are real, and Wilson and company have been correct all along. The fact remains, however, that discursive and material practices that engender distrust, fear, greed, selfishness, and competition only enliven such leanings. This much is known with certainty. We still have to foster human relations that engender empathy, cooperation, diversity, and equality. The fact that human beings possess a proclivity for aggression by no means represents an endorsement of the status quo. Yet proponents of the status quo get away with this sleight-of-hand argument. I have sought to show that the possibility for cooperation, equality, and diversity resides within human beings.

Epilogue

A nonhierarchical worldview challenges popular notions of God. It deligitimizes hierarchy as something sacred. If communion with the world and other beings requires liberation, then how could God design human beings both for liberation and hierarchy? In other words, with regard to redemption and functional human relations, how could God ordain both the ways of liberation and oppression?

Such questions have tortured persons of faith. The answers have been anything but convincing. For example, John Haught, Professor and Chairperson of the Theology Department at Georgetown University, deals with the matter in the following way:

> For by submitting to teachings and ethical norms, won't we give up our freedom, and thereby the kind of life in Christ and the Spirit that St. Paul equates with redemption? . . . The question of how to balance our personal freedom with the life of following a teacher and living in community is not only a Christian concern. It is one that all humans face. (1997, p. 7)

Haught then resorts—almost literally—to a *deus ex machina*:

> A perfect balance of freedom and following remains elusive, but we can find encouragement in our hope for the coming of the kingdom of God. God's kingdom implies a situation wherein freedom is no longer in tension with discipleship. (p. 7)

Haught misses the fact that liberation is the only path to communion with the world. Liberation requires human relations devoid of domination and subordination. Such relations show that our own becoming is related to the becoming of the world. Indeed, our existential strivings reflect a yearning to find oneness or wholeness with the consciousness of the world. Consequently, no tension or contradiction exists between the ways of liberation and redemption. No *deus ex machina* is necessary.

Haught also believes that liberation means autonomy. This equation reduces liberation to promiscuity, recklessness, and selfishness. It negates the fact that our humanity emerges through community. It constrains our responsibility to others by emasculating our connectedness. It also misses the fact that liberation is an artifact of human and collective development. In short, by equating liberation and autonomy Haught only sustains the unnecessary tension between submission and liberation. Consequently, his troubles are many:

> On the other hand we have to be followers simply in order to fulfill our human need to belong—to family, community, nation, church or other social groupings. On the other hand, we also need to be ourselves. If we try too hard to belong, we lose ourselves and our freedom. But if we strive to free ourselves from communion with others, we forfeit the sense of shared meaning also essential to human vitality. How shall we find deliverance from this predicament? (p. 7)

Haught leaves coercion uninterrogated. Consequently, he believes that redemption demands submission. However, by leaving coercion uninterrogated, Haught forecloses on other conceptualizations of God, liberation, and our relations to the world. He aptly showcases the point made at the beginning of this project. That is, discussions about liberation suffer from too many uninterrogated assumptions. Again, all worldviews posit various notions of the world, and such notions bear directly on what liberation means.

Accordingly, when bedrock assumptions go uninterrogated, the effect is a resorting to various ploys to plug structural contradictions. Consequently, Haught must resort to a faith based on belief rather than enlightenment. He hopes for the coming of God. The emergent paradigm makes for a faith that is consistent with emergent truths of the world. It neither fragments our humanity nor engenders a fear of the unknown or the other. It commits us to act purposely and spontaneously upon the world so as to bring forth the abundant potentiality that rests herein.

A new synthesis is granting the status quo further legitimacy. I refer to this new synthesis as the New Enlightenment. It merges propositions of the emergent paradigm, natural selection theory, and the mathematization (rational modeling) of human behavior; or, a trinity of physics, biology, and mathematics. Undoubtedly this is a superficially convincing arrangement because the *hard* sciences are seen by many as the guardians of Truth. Accordingly, behind the cloak of supposed rigor and objectivity, along with the mysticism of endless numerical equations ("Proofs of The Theoretical Propositions"), the hard sciences are being used to support the status quo in claiming that emergent "truths" reveal that the physics of the good society are embodied in market forces. The success of this argument can be seen in the new popularity of recent appropriations of natural selection theory to explain human behavior. Debates about the virtues of market forces have been subtly moved from the *soft* sciences to the *hard* sciences. It is made to seem that to enter the discussion knowing the ways of the hard sciences is compulsory. This ploy silences many dissenting voices. Moreover, the way that the argument is now articulated, any criticism of the status quo is seen as questioning the authority of the hard sciences. In this way, the hard sciences now function as both sword and shield for the status quo.

This New Enlightenment poses serious concerns. It now shapes a lot of governmental policy, particularly deregulation. The notion that chaos is fecund is now used to defend the unleashing of market forces. Natural selection theory is ubiquitous. Witness the celebration of competition and the endless calls for increasing the conditions that foster competition. Witness also the ostensibly moral defenses of the consequences of competition. Competition is cast as possessing natural correcting forces that will organically propel us to the good society. Supposedly, gains gotten from competition are purely the result of the best and the brightest rising to the top.

Inequality is morally legitimized. George Will, a nationally syndicated columnist, writes:

> A society that values individualism, enterprise and a market economy is neither surprised nor scandalized when the unequal distribution of marketable skills produces large disparities in the distribution of wealth. This does not mean that social justice must be defined as whatever distribution of wealth the market produces. But it does mean there is a presumption in favor of respecting the market's version of distributive justice. Certainly there is today no prima facie case against the moral acceptability of increasingly large disparities of wealth. (1995, p. A15)

The contest for survival supposedly makes for a natural hierarchy that accurately reflects differences and makes for a natural ordering that is vital for the survival and well-being of all. Again, the brightest, fittest, and strongest rise to the top and others less so fall accordingly to the bottom. Hierarchy supposedly represents natural goodness, fairness, and justice. The apparent purity of natural selection theory actually has provoked many members of traditionally disadvantaged and disenfranchised groups to extol the virtues of competition and to admonish supposed parasites seeking a life sustained on the gains of others. The purity deflects scrutiny and criticism away from the status quo. Our scorn is reserved for those who supposedly want something for nothing. Our wrath is for those posing a threat to the status quo by promoting habits of being and politics that undercut market forces and a consciousness distilled from such forces.

To speak of the possibility of liberation is different from speaking of the reality of liberation. Liberation is a process rather than an end. It exists only between human beings. Liberation represents the most profound expression of being human. The reality of liberation depends on our willingness to confront the world genuinely and transparently. It requires us to suspend our deep distrust and suspicion of the world and our own humanity. It requires us to struggle with the trials and tribulations of constructing deep and meaningful human relations. It is a difficult journey. It is risky. We have to risk life. In the end, this is what matters most. Liberation is the currency of redemption.

References

Abel, E. L., & Buckley, B. E. (1977). *The handwriting on the wall*. Westport, CT: Greenwood Press.

Alexander, B. (1978). Male and female rest room graffiti. *The International Journal of Verbal Aggression, 2*, 42-59.

Angell, R. C. (1965). The sociology of human conflict. In E. McNeil (Ed.), *The nature of human conflict*. Englewood Cliffs, NJ: Prentice-Hall.

Axelrod, R. (1984). *The evolution of cooperation*. New York: Basic Books.

Babrow, A. S. (1993). The advent of multiple-process theories of communication. *Journal of Communication, 43*, 110-118.

Baruch Bush, R. A., & Folger, J. P. (1994). *The promise of mediation*. San Francisco: Jossey-Bass.

Barnett, G. A. (1988). Communication and organizational culture. In G.M. Goldhaber & G.A. Barnett (Eds.), *Handbook of organizational communication* (pp. 101-130). Norwood, NJ: Ablex.

Beatty, M. J., & McCroskey, J. C. (1997). It's in our nature: Verbal aggressiveness as temperamental expression. *Communication Quarterly, 45*, 446-460.

Beatty, M. J., & McCroskey, J. C. (1998). Interpersonal communication as temperamental expression: A communibiological paradigm. In J. C. McCroskey, J. A. Daly, M. M. Martin, & M. J. Beatty (Eds.), *Communication and personality: Trait perspectives* (pp. 41-67). Cresskill, NJ: Hampton Press.

Beisecker, T. (1970). Game theory in communicative research: A reaction and a reorientation. *Journal of Communication, 20*, 105-120.

Blotchy, A. D., Carscanddon, D. M., & Grandmaison, S. L. (1983). Self-disclosure and physical health: In support of curvilinearity. *Psychological Reports, 53*, 903-906.

Bohm, D. (1980). *Wholeness and the implicate order*. New York: Routledge.

Bonello, C. G. (1992). Participatory democracy and the dilemma of social change. In L. Krimerman, F. Lindenfeld, C. Korty, & J. Benello (Eds.), *From the ground up* (pp. 37-48). Boston: South End Press.

Bonuso, C.A. (1976). Graffiti. *Today's Education, 65*, 90-91.

Bookchin, M. (1980). *Toward an ecological society*. Cheektowaga, NY: Black Rose Books.

Bookchin, M. (1995). *Re-enchanting humanity*. New York: Cassell.

Bork, R. (1996). *Slouching towards Gomorrah*. New York: Regan Books.

Bostrom, B. (1968). Game theory in communicative behavior. *Journal of Communication, 18*, 379-387.

Boyd, S. R. (1981). The cultural differences of female graffiti. *Journal of the Metropolitan Washington Communication Association, 9*, 25-38.

Briggs, J. L. (1970). *Never in anger: Portrait of an Eskimo family*. Cambridge, MA: Harvard University Press.

Brooks-Gunn, J., Klebanov, P. K., Liaw, F., & Spiker, D. (1993). Enhancing development of low-birthweight, premature infants: Change cognition and behavior over the first three years. *Child Development, 64*, 736-753.

Brown, W. K. (1978). Graffiti, identity, and the delinquent gang. *International Journal of Offender Therapy and Comparative Criminology, 22*, 46-48.

Bruner, E. M., & Kelso, J. P. (1980). Gender differences in graffiti: A semiotic perspective. *Women's Studies International Quarterly, 3*, 239-252.

Burawoy, M., & Wright, O. E. (1990). Coercion and consent in contested exchange. *Politics & Society, 18*, 251-266.

Carr, C. L. (1988). Coercion and freedom. *American Philosophical Quarterly, 25*, 59-65.

Chelune, G. J. (1989). Marital intimacy and self-disclosure. *Journal of Clinical Psychology, 39,* 463-474.

Chomsky, N. (1987). Language and freedom. In J. Peck (Ed.), *The Chomsky reader* (pp. 139-156). New York: Pantheon Books.

Clastres, P. (1989). *Society against the state.* New York: Zone Books.

Clegg, R. C. (1989). *Frameworks of power.* Newbury Park, CA: Sage.

Clegg, S. (1994). Social theory for the study of organizations: Weber and Foucault. *Organization, 1,* 149-178.

Cole, C. M. (1991). "Oh wise women of the stalls . . ." *Discourse & Society, 2,* 401-411.

Cox, T. H., Lobel, S. A., & McLeod, P. L. (1991). Effects of ethnic group cultural differences on cooperative and competitive behavior on a group task. *Academy of Management Journal, 34,* 827-847.

Davis, D. K., & Jasinski, J. (1993). Beyond the culture wars: An agenda for research on communication and culture. *Journal of Communication, 43,* 141-149.

Dawkins, R. (1989). *The selfish gene.* Oxford: Oxford University Press.

Deetz, S. (1992). *Democracy in an age of corporate colonization.* Albany: State University of New York Press.

Deetz, S. (1995). *Transforming communication, transforming business.* Cresskill, NJ: Hampton Press.

Deetz, S., & Kersten, S. (1983). Critical models of interpretive research. In L. Putnam and M. Pacanowsky (Eds.), *Communication and organizations* (pp. 147-171). Beverly Hills, CA: Sage.

Deiulio, A. M. (1978). Of adolescent cultures and subcultures. *Educational Leadership, 35,* 518- 520.

Dennett, D. C. (1995). *Darwin's dangerous idea.* New York: Simon & Schuster.

de Waal, F. B. M. (1997, June 27). Bonobos are from Venus. *The Chronicle of Higher Education,* B7-B9.

Deutsch, M. (1969). Conflicts: Productive and destructive. *Journal of Social Issues, 25,* 7-41.

Dundes, A. (1966). Here I sit—A study of American latrinalia. *Kroeber Anthropological Society Papers, 34,* 91-105.

Durmuller, U. (1986). Research on mural sprayscripts (graffiti). In A. R. Thomas (Ed.), *Methods in dialectology.* Clevedon, UK: Multilingual Matters.

Durmuller, U. (1988). Sociolinguistic aspects of mural sprayscripts (graffiti). *Sociolinguistics, 17,* 1-16.

Ehring, D. (1989). Are workers forced to work? *Canadian Journal of Philosophy, 9*, 589-602.

Farrington D. P. (1994). Early developmental prevention of juvenile delinquency. *Criminal Behavior and Mental Health, 4*, 209-227.

Feiner, J. S., & Klein, S.M. (1982, Winter). Graffiti talks. *Social Policy*, 47-53.

Fink, C. F. (1968). Some conceptual difficulties in the theory of social conflict. *Conflict Resolution, 12*, 412-460.

Fish, S. (1989). *Doing what comes naturally: Change, rhetoric, and practice of theory in literary and legal studies.* Durham, NC: Duke University Press.

Fraser, B. (1980). Meta-graffiti. *The International Journal of Verbal Aggression, 4*, 258-260.

Freire, P. (1993). *Pedagogy of the oppressed.* New York: Continuum.

Freud, S. (1961). *The future of an illusion.* New York: W. W. Norton.

Friedsam, H. (1964). Competition. In J. Gould & W. Kolb (Eds.), *A dictionary of the social sciences.* New York: Free Press of Glencoe.

Fromm, E. (1973). *The anatomy of human destructiveness.* New York: Henry Holt.

Fromm, E. (1976). *To have or to be.* New York: Continuum.

Fry, D. P. (1992). Respect for the rights of others is peace: Learning aggression versus non-aggression among the Zapotec. *American Anthropologist, 94*, 621-639.

Gadpaille, W. J. (1971). Graffiti: Its psychodynamic significance. *Sexual Behavior, 2*, 45-51.

Garcia, P. A., & Geisler, J. S. (1988). Sex and age/grade differences in adolescents' self-disclosure. *Perceptual and Motor Skills, 67*, 427-432.

Gaylin, W., & Jennings, B. (1996). *The perversion of autonomy.* New York: The Free Press.

Gibb, J. R. (1964). Climate for trust formation. In L.P. Bradford, J.R. Gibb, & K.D. Benne (Eds.), *T-group theory and laboratory method* (pp. 279-309). New York: Wiley.

Gielen, U. P. (1995). Traditional Buddhist Ladakh—A society at peace. In L. L. Adler & F. L. Denmark (Eds.), *Violence and the prevention of violence* (pp. 190-202). Westport, CT: Praeger.

Gilbert, M. (1993). Agreements, coercion, and obligation. *Ethics, 103*, 679-706.

Gilmar, S.T., & Brown, D. (1983). The final word on the bright adolescent or what to do with graffiti. *English Journal, 72*, 42-46.

Gladwell, M. (1997, March 3). Crime and science. *New Yorker*, 32-37.

Goldberg, S. (1993). *Why men rule.* Chicago: Open Court.

Gonzales, D. (1994, May). Death row. *VIBE*, 66-71.

Gorz, A. (1980). The scientist as worker. In R. Arditti, P. Brennan, & S. Cavrak (Eds), *Science and liberation* (pp. 267-280). Cheektowaga, NY: Black Rose Books.

Goswami, A. (1993). *The self-aware universe.* New York: Tarcher/Putnam Books.

Greenberg, M. A., & Stone, A.A. (1992). Emotional disclosure about traumas and its relation to health: Effects of previous disclosure and trauma severity. *Journal of Personality and Social Psychology, 63,* 75-84.

Gumpert, G. (1975). The rise of uni-comm. *Today's Speech, 23,* 34-38.

Hansen, J. E., & Schuldt, W. J. (1984). Marital self-disclosure and marital satisfaction. *Journal of Marriage and the Family, 12,* 923-926.

Hastings, R. (1984). Juve is majic: The anglicisms of Italian football graffiti. *Italian Studies, 39,* 91-102.

Haught, J. F. (1997, July 6). In freedom and fellowship. *The Catholic Moment,* 7.

Hentschel, E. (1987). Women's graffiti. *Multilingual Journal of Cross-Cultural and Interlanguage Communication, 6-3,* 287-308.

Herbert, W. (1997, April 21). Politics of biology. *U.S. News & World Report,* pp. 72-80.

Herrnstein, R. J., & Murray, C. (1994). *The bell curve.* New York: Free Press.

Hodson, J. D. (1983). *The ethics of legal coercion.* Dordrecht: D. Reidel.

Howell, S., & Willis, R. (1989). *Societies at peace: Anthropological perspectives.* London: Routledge.

Hubbard, R. (1998, July 3). Opinion. *The Chronicle of Higher Education,* B6.

Johnson, D. L., & Walker, T. (1987). Primary prevention of behavior problems in Mexican-American children. *American Journal of Community Psychiatry, 15,* 375-385.

Johnson, P. (1976). *A history of christianity.* New York: Atheneum.

Jones-Baker, D. (1981). The graffiti of folk motifs in Cotswold churches. *Folklore, 92,* 160-167.

Jourard, S. M. (1971). *The transparent self.* New York: Van Nostrand.

Keller, E. F. (1985). *Reflections on gender and science.* New Haven, CT: Yale University Press.

Kennedy, R. (1995). The phony war. In S. Fraser (Ed.), *The bell curve wars* (pp. 179-186). New York: Basic Books.

Klein, F. (1974). Commentary. In L. Gross (Ed.), *Sexual behavior: An interdisciplinary perspective* (pp. 87-88). New York: Spectrum.

Kohl, H. R. (1972). *Golden boy as Anthony Cool: A photo essay on naming and graffiti.* New York: Dial Press.

Kropotkin, P. (1989). *Mutual aid.* Cheektowaga, NY: Black Rose Books.

Kropotkin, P. (1992). *Ethics.* Cheektowaga, NY: Black Rose Books.

La Barre, W. (1979). Academic graffiti. *The International Journal of Verbal Aggression, 3,* 275-276.

Lally, J. R., Mangione, P. L., & Honig, A. S. (1988). Long-range impact of early intervention with low-income children and their families. In D. R. Powell (Ed.), *Parent education as early childhood intervention: Emerging directions in theory, research and practice* (pp. 79-104). Norwood, NJ, Ablex.

Larson, C. P. (1980). Efficacy of prenatal and postpartum home visits on child health and development. *Pediatrics, 66,* 191-197.

Lee, D. (1987). *Freedom and culture.* Prospects Heights, IL: Waveland Press.

Lewontin, R. C., Rose, S., & Kamin, L. J. (1984). *Not in our genes.* New York: Pantheon Books.

Ley, D., & Cybriwsky, R. (1974). Urban graffiti as territorial markers. *Annals of the Association of American Geographers, 64,* 491-505.

Lomas, H. D. (1976). Some clinical observations. *Psychoanalytic Review, 63,* 354-360.

Longnecker, G. J. (1977). Sequential parody graffiti. *Western Folklore, 36,* 354-360.

Lorde, A. (1984). *Sister outsider.* New York: The Crossing Press.

Lorenz, K. (1963). *On aggression.* Orlando, FL: Harcourt Brace.

Luna, G. C. (1987). Graffiti of homeless youth. *Society, 24,* 12-16.

Marion, R. (1992). Chaos, topology, and social organization. *Journal of School Leadership, 2,* 144-177.

McCroskey, J. C. (1998). *Why we communicate the ways we do: A communibiological perspective.* Needham, MA: Allyn and Bacon

McKercher, W. R. (1989). John Stuart Mill and liberty: A libertarian critique. In D. I. Roussopoulos (Ed.), *The anarchist papers 2* (pp. 51-106). Cheektowaga, NY: Black Rose Books.

McLaren, P. L., & Lankshear, C. (1994). Introduction. In P.L. McLaren & C. Lankshear (Eds.), *Politics of liberation* (pp. 1-11). New York: Routledge.

Melhorn, J. J., & Romig, R. J. (1985). Rest room: A descriptive study. *The Emporia State Research Studies, 34,* 29-45.

Misic, D. (1990). Fan identity symbols. *Kultura, 88-90,* 147-158. (From *Sociological Abstracts,* 1993, Abstract No.9303176).

Montagu, A. (Ed.). (1978). *Learning non-aggression. The experience of non-literate societies.* New York: Oxford University Press.

Mortensen, C. D. (1991). Communication, conflict, and culture. *Communication Theory, 4,* 273-293.

Mumby, D. K. (1997). Modernism, postmodernism, and communication studies: A rereading of an ongoing debate. *Communication Theory, 7,* 1-28.

Murray, M. J., & Dudrick, D. F. (1995). Are coerced acts free? *American Philosophical Quarterly, 32,* 109-123.

Nasar, S. (1998, June). A beautiful mind. *Vanity Fair,* 198-230.

Newall, V. (1986-1987). The moving spray can: A collection of some contemporary English graffiti. *The International Journal of Verbal Aggression, 9,* 39-47

Nicotera, A. M. (1993). Beyond two dimensions: A grounded theory model of conflict-handling behavior. *Management Communication Quarterly, 6,* 282-306.

Nicotera, A. M., & Rodriguez, A. J. (1994). *All fun but no games: The disappearance of game theory from the study of communication and conflict.* Paper presented at the annual meeting of the Western States Communication Association, San Jose, CA.

Nierenberg, J. (1983). Proverbs in graffiti: Taunting traditional wisdom. *The International Journal of Verbal Aggression, 7,* 41-58.

Norton, D. L. (1991). *Democracy and moral development.* Berkeley: University of California Press.

Opler, M. K. (1974). Commentary. In L. Gross (Ed.), *Sexual behavior: An interdisciplinary perspective* (pp. 86-87). New York: Spectrum.

Pennebaker, J. W., & Beall, A. K. (1986). Confronting a traumatic event: Towards an understanding of inhibitions and disease. *Journal of Abnormal Psychology, 95,* 274-281.

Prager, K. J. (1986). Intimacy status: Its relationship to locus of control, self-disclosure, and anxiety in adults. *Personality and Social Psychology Bulletin, 12,* 211-214.

Prigogine, I., & Stengers, I. (1984). *Order out of chaos: Man's dialogue with nature.* New York: Bantam Books.

Putnam, L., & Poole, M. S. (1987). Conflict and negotiation. In F.M. Jablin, L. Putnam, K.H. Robert & L.W. Porter (Eds.), *Handbook of organizational communication* (pp. 549-599). Newbury Park, CA: Sage.

Raine, A., Brennan, P., & Mednick, S. A. (1994). Birth complications combined with early maternal rejection at age 1 year predispose to violent crime at age 18 years. *Archives of General Psychiatry, 51,* 984-988.

Raine, A., Brennan, P., & Mednick, S. A. (1997). Interaction between birth complications and early maternal rejection in predisposing individuals to adult violence: Specificity to serious, early-onset violence. *American Journal of Psychiatry, 9,* 1265-1270.

Raine, A., Buchsbaum, M., & LaCasse, L. (1997). Brain abnormalities in murderers indicated by position emission tomography. *Biological Psychiatry, 42,* 495-508.

Raz, J. (1986). *The morality of freedom.* New York: Oxford University Press.

Reich, W., Buss, R., Fein, E., & Kurtz, T. (1977). Notes on women's graffiti. *Journal of American Folklore, 90,* 188-191.

Reisner, R., & Wechsler, L. (1974). *Encyclopedia of graffiti.* New York: MacMillan.

Rodriguez, A., & Clair, R. P. (1999). Graffiti as communication: Exploring the discursive tensions of anonymous texts. *Southern Communication Journal, 65,* 1-15.

Russell, B. (1995). *Power: A new social analysis.* New York: Routledge.

Sahlins, M. (1976). *The use and abuse of biology: An anthropological critique of sociobiology.* Ann Arbor: The University of Michigan Press.

Seitz, V., Rosenbaum, L. K., & Apfel, N. H. (1985). Effects of family support intervention: A ten-year follow-up. *Child Development, 56,* 376-386.

Shulman, A. D. (1996). Putting group information technology in its place: Communication and good work group performance. In S. R. Clegg, C. Hardy, & W. R. Nord (Eds.), *Handbook of organization studies* (pp. 357-374). London: Sage.

Shulman, B. H., Peven, D., & Byrne, A. (1973). Graffiti therapy. *Hospital and Community Psychiatry, 24,* 339-340.

Sidman, M. (1989). *Coercion and its fallout.* Boston: Authors Cooperative.

Smith, W. (1995). *The quantum enigma.* Peru, IL: Sherwood Sugden.

Spann, S. (1973). The handwriting on the wall. *English Journal, 62,* 1163-1165.

Spence, L. D. (1978). *The politics of social knowledge.* University Park: The Pennsylvania State University Press.

Spretnak, C. (1991). *States of grace.* New York: Harper & Row.

Steinfatt, T. M., & Miller, G. R. (1974). Communication in game theoretic models of conflict. In G. R. Miller & H. W. Simmons (Eds.), *Perspectives on communication in social conflict* (pp. 14-71). Englewood Cliffs, NJ: Prentice Hall.

Stiles, W.B., Shuster, P.L., & Harrigan, J.H. (1992). Disclosure and anxiety: A test of the fever model. *Journal of Personality and Social Psychology, 63,* 980-988.

Symons, D. (1990). *The evolution of human sexuality.* New York: Oxford University Press.

Thayer, L. (1973). Toward an ethics of communication. In L. Thayer (Ed.), *On communication: Essays in understanding.* Norwood, NJ: Ablex.

Thayer, L. (1997). *Pieces: Toward a revisioning of communication/life.* Greenwich, CT: Ablex.

Therborn, G. (1980). *The ideology of power the power of ideology.* London: Verso.

Tolstedt, B. E., & Stokes, J. P. (1984). Self-disclosure, intimacy, and the depenetration process. *Journal of Personality and Social Psychology, 46,* 84-90.

Tompkins, P. K., & Cheney, G. (1985). Communication and unobtrusive control in contemporary organizations. In R.D. McPhee & P.K. Tompkins (Eds.), *Organizational communication: Traditional themes and new directions* (pp. 179-210). Beverly Hills, CA: Sage.

Turner, C. G., & Turner, J. A. (1999). *Man corn: Cannibalism and violence in the prehistoric American Southwest.* Salt Lake City: The University of Utah Press.

Vervort, L., & Lievens, S. (1989). Graffiti in sports centers: An exploratory study in East Flanders. *Tijdsch Rift-Voor-Sociale-Wetenschappen, 34,* 56-53.

Waller, B. N. (1990). *Freedom without responsibility.* Philadelphia: Temple University Press.

Wallerstein, I. (1992). The challenge of maturity. *Review, 15,* 1-7.

Weiger, W.A., & Bear, D.M. (1988). An approach to the neurology of aggression. *Journal of Psychiatry Residency, 22,* 85-95.

Weissberg, R. (1999). *Political tolerance.* Thousand Oaks, CA: Sage.

Wertheimer, A. (1988). *Coercion.* Princeton, NJ: Princeton University Press.

Will, G. (1995, April 24). What's behind income disparity. *San Francisco Chronicle,* p. A 15.

Wilson, E. O. (1975, October 12). Human decency is animal. *The New York Times Magazine,* pp. 38-50.

Wilson, E. O. (1978). *On human nature.* Cambridge, MA: Harvard University Press.

Wilson, E. O. (1980). *Sociobiology* (Abridged edition). Cambridge, MA: The Belknap Press.

Wilson, E. O. (1998). *Consilience: The unity of knowledge*. New York: Knopf.

Witteman, M. (1991). Group member satisfaction: A conflict related account. *Small Group Research, 22*, 24-58.

Wolfe, A. (1993). *The human difference*. Berkeley: University of California Press.

Wrangham, R., & Peterson, D. (1996). *Demonic males: Apes and the origins of human violence*. Boston: Houghton Mifflin.

Wright, R. (1994). *The moral animal: The new science of evolutionary psychology*. New York: Vintage.

Wright, W. (1998). *Born that way: Genes, behavior, personality*. New York: Knopf.

Young, R. Y. (1986). *Personal autonomy: Beyond and negative liberty*. New York: St. Martin's Press.

Young, T. R. (1991). Chaos theory and symbolic interaction theory: Poetics for the postmodern sociologist. *Symbolic Interaction, 14*, 321-334.

Young, T. R. (1992). Chaos theory and human agency: Humanist sociology in a postmodern era. *Humanity & Society, 16*, 441-460.

Zagare, F. C. (1984). *Game theory: Concepts and applications*. Newbury Park, CA: Sage.

Zimmerman, M. E. (1994). *Contesting earth's future*. Berkeley: University of California Press.

Author Index

Kurtz, T., 60, *120*

L

La Barre, W., 59, *118*
LaCasse, L., 37, *120*
Lally, J.R., 39, *118*
Lankshear, C., 26, *118*
Larson, C.P., 39, *118*
Lee, D., 102, *118*
Lewontin, R.C., 67, 68, 69, *118*
Ley, D., 59, *118*
Liaw, F., 39, *114*
Lievens, S., 59, *121*
Lobel, S.A., 43, 95, *115*
Lomas, H.D., 58, *118*
Longnecker, G.J., 58, *118*
Lorde, A., 99, 100, *118*
Lorenz, K., 35, *118*
Luna, G.C., 59, *118*

M

Mangione, P.L., 39, *114*
Marion, R., 84, *118*
McCroskey, J.C., 65, 66, 67, 68, *113*, *118*
McKercher, W.R., 37, *119-120*
McLaren, P., 26, *118*
McLeod, P.L., 43, 95, *115*
Mednick, S.A., 37, *119-120*
Melhorn, J.J., 59, *118*
Miller, G.R., 41, 44, 47, *120*
Misic, D., 59, *118*
Montagu, A., 39, *119*
Mortensen, C.D., 19, 94, *119*
Mumby, D.K., 23, 24, *119*
Murray, C., 64, *117*
Murray, M.J., 5, *119*

N

Nasar, S., 41, *119*
Newall, V., 59, *119*
Nicotera, A.M., 48, 95, *119*
Nierenberg, J., 58, *119*
Norton, D.L., 104, *119*

O

Opler, M.K., 59, *119*

P

Pennebaker, J.W., 60, 99, *119*
Peterson, D., 71, *122*
Peven, D., 61, *120*
Poole, M.S., 94, 95, *120*
Prager, K.J., 99, *120*
Prigogine, I., 74, *120*
Putnam, L., 94, 95, *120*

R

Raine, A., 37, *119-120*
Raz, J., 3, *120*
Reich, W., 60, *120*
Reisner, R., 59, *120*
Rodriguez, A.J., 48, 59, 119, *120*
Romig, R.J., 59, *118*
Rose, S., 67, 69, *118*
Rosenbaum, L.K., 39, *120*
Russell, B., 18, *120*

S

Sahlins, M., 51, 95, *120*
Schuldt, W.J., 99, *117*
Seitz, V., 39, *120*
Shulman, A.D., 105, *120*
Shulman, B.H., 61, 105, *120*
Shuster, P.L., 60, 99, *121*
Sidman, M., 6, *120*
Smith, W., 79, 80, 81, *120*
Spann, S., 59, *120*
Spence, L.D., 17, 91, *120*
Spiker, D., 39, *114*
Spretnak, C., 52, *120*
Steinfatt, T.M., 41, 44, 47, *120*
Stengers, I., 74, *120*
Stiles, W.B., 60, 99, *121*
Stokes, J.P., 99, *121*
Stone, A.A., 60, 99, *117*
Symons, D., 50, *121*

T

Thayer, L., 11, 50, 105, 106, *121*

Therborn, G., 73, *121*
Tolstedt, B.E., 99, *121*
Tompkins, P.K., 7, *121*
Turner, C.G., 36, *121*
Turner, J.A., 36, *121*

V

Vervort, L., 59, *121*

W

Walker, T., 39, *117*
Waller, B.N., 5, *119*
Wallerstein, I., 83, 84, *121*
Wechsler, L., 59, *120*
Weiger, W.A., 37, *121*
Weissberg, R., 19, *121*
Wertheimer, A., 5, *119*

Will, G., 112, *122*
Willis, R., 39, *117*
Wilson, E.O., 32, 33, 34, 35, 36, 49, *121, 122*
Witteman, M., 95, 96, *122*
Wolfe, A., 27, 48, 71, *122*
Wrangham, R., 71, *122*
Wright, O.E., 5, *114*
Wright, R., 54-55, *122*

Y

Young, T.R., 5, 83, *122*

Z

Zagare, F.C., 41, *122*
Zimmerman, M., 20, *122*

Subject Index